"Crossing the Mediterra
exploration of the roots of so.... .. .. o-.. ...... .ns.
Ms. Stone's writing is sensitive and insightful, and her accounts
of experiences always tinged with humor.
A real pleasure from beginning to end."

— Dan Parlow, President of MyTripJournal.com

"This memoir captures an authentic life experience—a journey
to fascinating places and an insight into the mind of the author.
With interesting points of view and unexpected events, this
adventure is a real eye opener."

— Filip V., Founder of WorldTravelStories.com

" . . . "

— Anonymous Travel Magazine

(Some refined travel magazines, promoting sophisticated world travel to wealthy, politically-correct
American tourists, prefer not to be associated with my more honest and open approach to writing.)

"Her best work yet!"

— Laura Stone (Me)

The world is a book authored by God,

and those who never travel, read only a page.

Crossing the Mediterranean:
Finding Myself Abroad

Journeys of a SandSeeker

Laura Stone

Crossing the Mediterranean: Finding Myself Abroad

Cover and interior art created by
Laura Stone Studios

253 Sponsel Branch
Vanceburg, KY 41179

ISBN 978-0-557-05182-3

I dedicate this book to the two most important women in my life:
my mom, Barbara Stone, and my sister, Sarah Stone Mawk,
for helping me remember my Northeastern Kentucky roots,
while exploring cultural diversity worldwide.
I could never forget *who* I am.
Thank you.

Don't Miss Other Adventures by Laura Stone:

"I Give Seven Chicken": And Other Travel Experiences in China
ISBN 978-1-4303-1001-3 (paperback)

Whether you're currently planning a trip to Beijing or dabbling with the idea of visiting the Great Wall during your lifetime, Laura Stone's travel memoir is a must read. *"I Give Seven Chicken": And Other Travel Experiences in China*, provides readers with a sense of how it actually feels for American tourists to be immersed into Chinese culture. Most published works available on China provide only factual travel information, but they do not include personal stories that intimately describe the Chinese culture through Western eyes. Most definitely, the experiences shared in this book document a hilarious culture clash of West meets East!

Americans in Brasil: "Isn't it spelled with a 'z'?"
ISBN 978-0-557-00883-4 (paperback)

Would you like to know what the travel magazines are leaving out? Travel with Laura Stone to South America from the comfort of your living room. No need to worry about fending off thieves, meeting your death in piranha infested waters, or tiptoeing past machinegun-wielding guards. The author has experienced all this for you. Sit back, relax, and envision the iconic sights of Brazil, including the Amazon rainforest, Sugarloaf Mountain, and Christ the Redeemer statue. Imagine a panoramic waterfall much grander than Niagara on the Argentinean border. Dare to enter Paraguay. Learn about the cultures of these regions, as the author works her way around the continent, observing and interacting with customs outside her own. Allow yourself to become spoiled by her honesty, openness, and humor. Besides, the book is much cheaper than the airfare! Are you ready for the journey to begin?

Available at Amazon.com

TABLE OF CONTENTS

"Trip Map"

DISCLAIMER

This is not a coffee table travel book. There are no embellished descriptions of foreign places to inspire blank smiles. Travel can be hard work, and there are always unavoidable mishaps along the way. I'm not going to leave out the juicy details! These can be some of the most valuable learning experiences.

Also, I call things exactly as I see them. No effort has been made to force negative experiences into politically correct molds. Why try? If my encounters support a stereotype, then that's exactly the way it is. The good, the bad, and the ugly are addressed in this memoir. Prepare yourself, or step away.

Travel is one of my greatest passions, and I love *honestly* recording my findings. Without exception, I would relive every trip that I have ever taken. I enjoy learning about new ways of life and adapting my perspectives as I explore the globe. This doesn't mean that I cherish every aspect of all the cultures of the world. That's nonsense! I integrate the aspects that please me and leave the rest behind. By the end of my life, I would like to be a personal patchwork of the best the world has to offer.

My favorite hobby is collecting sand because it serves as an organic reminder of each nation I visit. These symbolic granules hold a special place in my heart because they represent their respective countries, along with all the people and the customs that I've encountered along the way. The colors of the sand range from the deepest blacks to the purest whites, with a multitude of grays, browns, and pinks in between; the granules are at least as varied and diverse as the people that live there. Thus, I manage to take a little piece of every country home with me, both literally and figuratively. That's why I call myself a SandSeeker.

INTRODUCTION

I have always had a fascination for culture. At the age of five, I can remember singing Spanish songs with Sesame Street characters. I loved learning, and anything different enthralled me. As I grew older, I started traveling. I desired to immerse myself into foreign environments. Visiting China, Japan, the Caribbean, Brazil, Argentina, and Paraguay thrilled me. I could not experience enough. I longed to know more, to understand more, to live more. Even though I didn't always correctly interpret what I was observing, I yearned to be a part of it. I sought to experience diversity, to appreciate the many aspects of humanity. I wanted to swallow the world.

Discovering new things became a priority. The more I experienced, the more I craved. I developed a deep appreciation for culture, which in turn nurtured a love for *all* of God's creations. Sometimes, I found myself thinking that this must be the way God views us, his interesting and unique children. He must enjoy watching us, entertained by how varied we are within our groups. This must be why he crafted each of us so distinctly—to make us more delightful in his eyes.

On previous trips to other countries, I had always looked for these differences, and relished them. This voyage across the Mediterranean, however, would be the first time that I would truly cast my gaze inward, instead of outward. By accident, I would take a journey of the heart. I would experience an intrapersonal quest for knowledge, far greater than I had anticipated.

I knew that I had planned a special voyage. First, I would be flying to Germany; then, I would cross Italy by train; and finally, I would sail to Egypt, Israel, Turkey, and Greece. I thought that this trip was going to be similar to my other globe-trotting experiences. I would explore interesting cultures, adapt some small aspects of my life, and come home virtually unchanged. But this isn't what happened. It's true that the world opened up to me, but it wasn't that simple. I didn't just see the world. I found myself.

LEAVING HOME

"I LOVE to travel, so *why* do I have this sinking feeling every time I leave the country?"

I was reprimanding myself as I closed the door of our house. No matter how much I travel, I always have butterflies in my stomach when it comes time to depart. It's not that I'm afraid to fly or scared to sail across the ocean. I find these modes of transportation alluring. The problem is my tugging heart strings. I have an unbreakable bond with my family, a connection to my motherland, and a fondness for my home that makes it difficult to leave. I feel as though I am stretching my emotional fabric across continents. It's painful. Yet, I am compelled to do so time and again. Travel has become my addiction. It's my pleasure source. It's my burden. I am driven to do it, and so I do. I pick up my heavy heart, focus on the highs, and consume the drug of travel.

I had planned this journey to the Mediterranean a year ago, and when the day finally arrived, I was buzzing with adrenaline. My husband Chad and I had loaded our luggage into the car the night before. The house was clean. Our bills were paid in advance. Everything was in place, but I could not shake my compounding anxiety. From the beginning, I had felt that there was something monumental about this trip. I just didn't know what it would be. The *unknown* factor was getting to me; I couldn't shake it.

On the way to the airport, I stopped to bid my mother farewell. She had been awake since dawn, and she was shoveling debris out of a ditch. The pouring rains from the night before had clogged them with mud, leaves, and stones. I paused to watch her. She was covered in dried mud; her curlers were tightly wound with her thin blonde hair, and her glasses occasionally slipped down the sweaty slope of her nose. She was beautiful. I would always remember her this way, working until her back would almost break in order to have everything right and proper in our world. She heaved a massive shovelful of gravel into a wheelbarrow as I approached her from behind.

"I'm leaving now," I announced.

She turned to acknowledge me. "You are?" There was concern in her words. She knew where I was headed, and it troubled her. She always worried about me, but she especially fretted when I was overseas. "You better be careful," she warned.

"I will," I promised, digging the toe of my shoe into the damp dirt driveway to form a tiny indentation. I wanted to confess how much I would miss her—that I would take her with me if I could. I would take this whole farm with me if I could. But it was a silly thing to say. Besides, she already knew. Saying it out loud would be foolish because such things were not possible. She wasn't going anywhere. I would have a better chance of folding up the entire farm and sticking it into my pocket than getting her to agree to come with me.

"I'll see you when you get back," she spoke softly, her voice quivering just a little.

"Yeah," I whispered and held out my arms.

She embraced me, and we both started to cry. I felt good in her arms. She had always made me feel safe, loved, cared for. For a second, I didn't want to leave. I wanted to absorb her love forever, but like so many things, this wasn't possible. I squeezed her tight, and then we released our embrace. We looked at each other, wiping our eyes. No words were needed. We were both afraid that we might never see one another again. Sure, the chances of a plane crash, heart attack, or suicide bomber were all ridiculously low, but the statistics didn't eliminate the concern.

We rubbed the tears away and looked at each other again. Then, we burst out into laughter at how depressing we were both being.

"I will be back!" I proclaimed a bit more cheery.

Mom nodded, smiled, and went back to shoveling. My journey had begun. I had said my good-byes, and now I was off to see the world—or at least the Mediterranean.

"Ma and Pa Sponsel with My Grandpa Howard Reis"

FINDINGS IN FRANKFURT

It is a rarity in my travels to visit a place and feel a true kinship to the land and its people. I have never "fit in" while abroad. Most likely, this is because I decided to investigate Asia and South America prior to venturing into Europe. Although I thoroughly enjoyed myself on these diverse continents, there had been many aspects of these cultures that had perplexed me. I couldn't have imagined crowding mob-style in front of a ticket counter, for instance, until I witnessed the custom first-hand in China. Nor could I have envisioned the passionate live-for-the-moment lifestyle that I had observed in Brazil. I was much too restrained and orderly; so many of these day-to-day practices were foreign to me. I had always felt like an outsider. But on this trip, I discovered something completely unexpected. I found a little of myself in my surroundings.

It seems strange to think that I would have to travel across the ocean to better understand my own character, but that's what happened. I will have to share a bit of my background in order to better explain these discoveries.

As a child, I had listened to stories about my grandpa's great-grandfather, Joseph Friedrich Reis [pronounced Rice], who had traveled with his family from the state of Würtemberg in southwest Germany during the late 1840s. I fantasized, in my young mind, about what his journey must have been like, leaving his home, friends, and extended family behind. He most likely sailed for weeks on a ship, crossing the Atlantic to an unfamiliar land. I had learned that sometimes two to three thousand people were crammed onto these immigrant steamships, which were hardly adequate to accommodate a thousand passengers. Cleanliness, privacy, and comfort took a back seat to cheap transportation. Upon arrival in America, he agreed to change his name to Joseph Reis [pronounced Reese] because it was deemed more appropriate by those in the new land. This was the first of many adjustments he would make to Americanize himself. The voyage must have been an extraordinarily difficult, sad, and terrifying time for Joseph. I tried to imagine what formidable conditions would bring someone to abandon his life, leave everything behind, and set out for the unknown.

As I grew older, I began to investigate historical texts, and I have managed to piece together a rough understanding of Joseph's plight. According to my research, there was much upheaval in Germany during the eighteenth and nineteenth centuries. War and political unrest had plagued the country for years. Beginning in the 1700s, a flood of immigration transpired in response to insufferable brutalities. German citizens were being attacked by soldiers of various nationalities. Inhabitants of the southwest region, in particular, were being constantly robbed and tortured, sometimes with entire villages being slaughtered and burned to the ground. One such episode occurred in 1707, when a French army under the leadership of Marshal Villars crossed the Rhine and plundered throughout the region. Certainly, my relatives would have been affected by these traumas. More than likely, Joseph grew up listening to ancestral tales of death and destruction (similar to the way I heard about his journey and relocation).

Then, in the 1800s, modernization and population growth forced many Germans from their family businesses. This economic downturn made unsettling times even more unbearable. The failed German revolution of 1848 stimulated another massive movement to America. In a single decade, over one million Germans relocated to the United States. Many of these Germans, including Joseph, settled in the Cincinnati area.

From my reading, I could understand why Joseph left Germany. Like so many others, he desired to make a better life for himself in a homeland that was founded on the promises of freedom and peace. I am deeply impressed with my ancestor's determination and commitment to change. Life was difficult for him—perhaps even more so than he had anticipated.

Cincinnati, at that time, was becoming a major pork-processing center, and the job market for working-class immigrants was booming. In an area known as Over-the-Rhine, Germans settled into a tight-knit community with their own churches, schools, and German-language newspapers. However, other Cincinnati residents blamed the Germans for many of the city's problems. The locals were upset because the immigrants were seizing much-needed jobs. Employers favored immigrants because they could pay them less than other workers.

Collectively, working-class immigrants were viewed by the public as diseased, feeble-minded, and inferior. Often stereotyped and discriminated against, many Germans suffered verbal and physical abuse because they were different and unpopular. They found themselves ridiculed by the public, from comic strips to laws that affected only Germans. The social stigma became so detrimental that children, who were the sons and daughters of immigrants, would be embarrassed of their heritage and focus on assimilating.

Most likely, this pressure to conform is what led to the eventual loss of the German language in my own family. It takes effort to discard a language and adopt another tongue, and my grandpa, Howard Reis, was the first generation to speak English without a German accent. His great-grandfather, Joseph Reis, had been comfortably fluent in only the German language upon arriving in America. Most likely, Joseph's son, Charles Friedrich "Henry" Reis, learned to speak both English and German to some degree. Henry's son, George Reis, was able to speak fluent English, but with a strong German influence. Because George's father had died so young, his mother had remarried another German man by the name of John Sponsel. Mr. Sponsel had more recently made his way to America. After fighting in the Franco-Persian war, he had gained his American citizenship in August 1878. Definitely, George's vocabulary and diction were heavily influenced by his new step-father, who spoke fluent German. However, George's son, my grandpa, grew up speaking English, without a trace of our German past. Any tidbits of German that he might have known were lost, as he passed nothing along to my mother. Thus, I speak no German whatsoever. I always thought that losing such a large piece of our family history was a shame, yet I have developed an understanding of why it came to pass. Americanization was of utmost importance to my ancestors. Today, I also realize why my family left Cincinnati.

I believe that my forbearers, like most newcomers, felt unwelcome by the established population. Social tensions continued to mount. In 1855, anti-German sentiments resulted in violence when a mob attempted to invade the German neighborhood. This aggression erupted into a three-day riot. German-American militia managed to fend off the attackers, but the continued conflicts caused many Germans to leave the city. The family of my great-grandfather, George Reis, was among those who sought contentment elsewhere. I can sympathize with the German disposition at this time; after all, they had left their

German homeland in order to live a quiet and undisturbed life in Cincinnati. Now, they were moving again to seek tranquility. In 1907, George Reis, his mother, siblings, and step-father moved 100 miles southeast of Cincinnati onto a farm in Northeastern Kentucky, where my family and I reside today.

Joseph, Henry, and George were characters from my past: my forefathers. Stories of these men had filled my childhood. They were the reason I existed, why I lived in America, and how I came to call our small farm near Cincinnati *home*. Yet, somehow they were more. Even at a young age, I realized that their German heritage had profoundly influenced my upbringing. In a vaguely inexplicable way, I knew that *they* were the reason lunch, the largest meal of the day, had to be served promptly at noon. *They* were why my mother had taught me to meticulously plan and anticipate every aspect of my life, striving to be as self-sufficient as possible. Because of *them*, I had grown into a reserved woman, who invited only close friends and family into the sanctity of my home. Punctual, intellectual, and self-motivated, their German influence had molded me into the person that I am. I found myself wondering how much of my personality had been affected by them and what other remnants of German culture lingered in my daily life. In June of 2008, I left the farm and became the first person in my family to return to Germany. It would turn out to be a very short, yet extremely insightful visit.

Even before landing in Germany, I felt exceptionally enthusiastic about "returning to the fatherland," as Uncle Michael had phrased it. Flying over the country, I could hardly believe my eyes! The earth below looked like home. The hills weren't as high, but there was a beloved, gentle rolling to the terrain. A tree-covered landscape provided a comforting lushness, similar to Appalachia. The view from my window could have been clipped from a Kentucky Living Magazine, yet I was far from the bluegrass state. I was in Deutschland. I imagined how delighted my ancestors, from farming descent, must have been to see the fields of Southern Ohio and Northeastern Kentucky, upon arriving from Germany. They surely would have been every bit as pleased as I was to behold such a familiar scene.

We touched down at the Frankfurt airport at 6:30 a.m. local time. The area surrounding the airport possessed a charming order. It was tidy, with everything in its place. There was a distinctly German atmosphere here. The Mock Tudor style buildings were enchanting, with their steeply pitched roofs, elongated windows, towering chimneys, and cream-colored walls crisscrossed by half-timbers. Without entering a single interior, I knew that the inside of each house sparkled with the spick-and span cleanliness of home. Their yards were immaculate, and it reminded me of the way mom trimmed and groomed everything so meticulously. The roads and structures were well-maintained, just as I thought they

"German Street"

should be. Few people were out at this early hour on Saturday, but those who were visible did not dilly-dally. Instead, everyone was rushing about, tending to matters of personal importance and minding their own business in the process. I found this highly-structured environment quite refreshing. In so many ways, my physical surroundings reflected my internal wiring.

And so, I began to realize that my long-time suspicions had been true. Much of my thinking and doing was German-influenced. Whether encoded into my genes or nurtured through my upbringing, my family history was helping me explain why I was so regimented, straightforward, persevering, and private. These were valued German traits that must have been passed down to me—ingrained into my very being.

My eyes continued to open. My ancestry was why I strove to be so analytical, literal, and precise! Order was of supreme importance. My German roots made it more difficult for me to leave a scrap of trash on the ground than to bend down and pick it up. My word was my honor, binding me to do as I said I would. Without my honor, I was worthless. These ideals came from Germany. I chose to do my best on every task, or I decided not to do it at all. All or nothing was my rule. This was German. Authority should be respected. Everyone in his place. I was thinking and acting like a German! It was so clear now. How could I have disregarded these connections for so long?

My Germanic characteristics were probably why I seemed so compulsive—like a perfectionist—to other Americans, and why I viewed many Americans as superficial and irresponsible. My German standards had been conflicting with my American environment. Thus, I was confirming what I had known in my heart to be true for years: my rearing had been dramatically German influenced, and these ideals had helped to form my personality.

Here, in Germany, I finally "fit-in." In fact, many people were mistaking me for a local. It felt oddly satisfying, but I knew that I was *not* a native. I had never lived in Germany, and I was never going to be a German. I was an American. This fact became painfully obvious when I spoke. My German vocabulary was beyond deficient, and this handicap would greatly hinder my information exchange. It wouldn't take long before everyone realized that I was authentically American. Sadly, my long list of linguistic complications began with a desire to write home.

This first communication challenge snapped me out of culture-analysis mode. I desperately wanted to email my sister Sarah to let her know that I had arrived safely. I forced my analytical daydreaming to cease, and concentrated my efforts. The easy part was finding an internet station (they were everywhere) and inserting my money. Once I had done that, the five minute pay-per-use countdown was on. I became serious and focused.

Unfortunately, I would soon realize that these available German facilities were not compatible with my American background. At first glance, the German keyboard appeared normal enough, with function keys across the first row, numbers under that, and letters that followed. I thought I could handle it. No problem, I could use a keyboard. Right? Upon closer inspection, I discovered—after 30 seconds of hunting—that the letter 'y' was missing. It was gone! Vanished! Where could it possibly have been hidden? Surely the letter 'y' existed in the German alphabet. I couldn't type my user name without it! I browsed over every button on the keyboard. Eventually, I realized that it was switched with the letter 'z'. Progress. One minute gone, and four minutes left. Determination was setting in.

Finally, I managed to log into my email account, and I typed a one-sentence notification that we had arrived. Eying the timer, I saw that I had already used a total of three minutes. Two minutes to go. All I had to do was type in my sister's email address and hit "send." This was doable, or so I thought. I began to type S-A-R-A-H . . . Where was the '@' symbol? I scanned hurriedly over the keyboard again, as the timer ticked away the seconds. It was on the 'Q' key. Why was it on a letter key, when it *should* be above the number two? I hit the button and mistakenly typed a lower case letter. NO! I need the '@' symbol not a 'q'! I held down the shift key and pressed the button, only to get a capital letter. Urgh! "Okay, the function key should do it," I thought. I tapped these two keys together, only to type another capital 'Q'! The 'ALT' key? This combination also resulted in a capital letter. Control key? Another capital letter. There was a minute left, and I was getting frantic. I turned to a Chinese man beside me, and asked him for help. Although he could speak English, he didn't know any more about German keyboards than I did.

"Did you try this," he suggested as he hit the 'ALT GR' key.

I don't even know what those letters stand for. It must be some sort of special German 'ALT'. Regardless, his attempt was to no avail, either. Another capital 'Q'. Out of frustration, I started pounding keys at random. Keys Ü, Ö, and Ä . . . what were these for? Letters with umlauts were useless to me and only served as annoyances. I watched as the seconds disappeared: 5, 4, 3, 2, and 1. Then, a giant screen flashed up, requesting that I insert more money. Not a chance! I gave up after a wasted five minutes, and I began to mourn the loss of my five dollars.

I would have cheered up in no time, if it hadn't been for another immediate German-language conundrum. To purchase train tickets, Chad and I needed to use a mechanical dispenser, but the directions were entirely in German. I don't mean easy German, either, with just city names as selections. There were two columns of buttons with over a dozen different German phrases in each column. I started reading the long list of choices. "Einzelfahrt nach Offenbach." What did that mean? "Hanau" and "Darmstadt." I didn't know. Were these cities? "Tageskarte Frankfurt Intel." This one was probably not right, since there was a picture of an airplane. I wanted to go to the city of Frankfurt, but the confusing list went on and on. Did I need a "wochenkarte"?

In almost a panic, I approached the information desk and asked how to purchase tickets into the city of Frankfurt. The young lady behind the counter named the button that I should press. I was so relieved that I turned immediately to do as she had instructed. As I twirled around to leave the line, I remembered that I had forgotten to ask how long the train ride would take. I wasn't fast enough. She was already assisting her next confused customer. At that moment, another woman came strolling out of the back office to form a second line of assistance. Perhaps I could ask her.

"Excuse me, how long is the train ride to Frankfurt?"

"No!" she bellowed. "First HELLO and then GOOD MORNING!"

Wow, I was completely taken aback. I hadn't thought that I had been rude at all. I smiled sheepishly, embarrassed that I had upset her so. "Hi," I managed to utter softly, trying this introduction thing again. Then, I gave her a subtle wave. "Do you know how long it takes to get to Frankfurt?"

She glared at me penetratively, paused, and replied flatly, "20 minutes."

"Thank you," I nodded, and then I disappeared.

All the way back to the ticket dispenser, my mind was consumed by what had just happened. Why had she been so abrupt with me? Maybe she disliked me because I was American; it was currently an unpopular nationality, with President Bush's controversial foreign policies. If this was the case, however, I wasn't going to let it bother me. My goodness, Germany was the root of the holocaust. Over six million Jews murdered! Last time I checked, America hadn't attempted to exterminate an entire race. She really didn't have much room for political criticisms. If I could overlook her national history, she should have been able to disregard mine. Besides, I didn't have any more to do with Guantanamo Bay or the war in Iraq than she had to do with concentration camps and WWII. Neither of us had ever been in charge of our governments.

The only nagging feeling was that perhaps this was not the reason she had snapped at me. Was it something else? Had I violated a sacred German custom that had not been passed down to me? I had no answer to these questions.

By the time I had reached the ticket machine, I had forgotten which button I was supposed to push. I stood blankly in front of the machine. Drats! Now what was I going to do, go back and face the testy Queen of Information? Groan. I strained at the keys, trying to remember the magic button that would take me to Frankfurt. It was no use. The valuable German phrase had slipped right out of my head. There was too much useless German bashing around up there. I still didn't know if I needed a "wochenkarte." What did that mean? I was never going to recall anything useful.

Luckily, the man behind me in line spoke a little English and was eager to move me out of his way. He pointed to the button that would take me to Frankfurt. I selected this option and tried to insert my money. To my surprise, the machine would not accept my bill. Over and over again, I attempted to feed the money into the slot. I looked at the note. The phrase "20 Euro," was printed on its front. Yep, it was German currency. I straightened it between my fingers, and poked it into the opening. The machine immediately spit it back out. Next, I polished it over the edge of the machine, hoping that the shiny box would grow fond of the bill's increased crispness. I tried again, but the dispenser coughed it up once more. I blew on it for good luck, and tried to slide it through. Again and again, the metallic orifice belched out my Euros. Alas, the ticket monster would not eat my money. Impatiently, the man behind me was repeating instructions in German. I guess he ran out of English. I had no choice but to step aside.

In less than three seconds, he had selected his destination, successfully deposited his cash, and was heading for the train platform. He didn't give me as much as a second glance. I was learning a lot about Germans, and undeniably, more than I wanted to recognize about myself. Was I that *efficient*? Could I accomplish all my tasks in no time flat, without regard to anyone else? I knew that I was guilty of it. With my head hung low, I returned to the "help desk."

"Hello. Good morning," I greeted the nicer woman behind the counter. The nasty Queen of Information was still scrutinizing my every word. I ignored her as best I could. "The machine is not taking my money to go to Frankfurt." I held up my bill for her inspection.

"Use a smaller one," she advised, with a "next-person-please" tone in her voice.

I returned to the machine, somewhat dumbfounded by her advice. One German after another was retrieving his ticket. As slick as a whistle, the money was sucked in and tickets dropped out. Finally, it was my turn in line. I made my city selection and punched a "10 Euro" bill into the mouth of the machine. Then, I squinted threateningly at the glistening silver box. What do you know? It worked! The machine slurped up my 10-value note, and out fell my tickets. Hurray!

"Now what do we do?" I turned and asked Chad.

"I suppose we wait for the train somewhere," he shrugged.

We both turned and looked at the numerous tracks that lay before us. Which one was *our* train? Aahhh. It was going to be a daunting task to find the right platform. I prepared myself for the indifference that was sure to come our way.

Then at that moment, the most bizarre event occurred. A German man motioned for us to follow him. Cautiously, we allowed him to lead us across the aisle and down an escalator. He pointed for us to stand there. Then, he dashed back up another set of stairs to the opposite side of the aisle and waited on his train. I was completely baffled. Had he just gone out of his way to help us? I gestured to him, slightly confused, pointing to my spot. "I am supposed to wait here," I summarized my interpretation. He nodded and pointed to his watch. Outstanding! He was telling me that I could board my train at this spot in only a few minutes! I waved happily to the helpful man. Seconds later, he climbed onto his train and vanished down the tracks.

Sure enough, our own train arrived within minutes, as he had promised. The glossy red car whisked us away to Frankfurt. All things considered, we had a very pleasant time in the city. Of course, I gathered a handful of German sand for my global sand

"Train Station, Frankfurt"

collection. I have a bottleful from every country I have visited. I was lucky enough to find a mound of powdery grains poured around the trunk of a tree, which had been planted in the sidewalk. Germany was country number 20! Precious granules collected, I decided to purchase a few common German souvenirs, including a beer stein magnet, scenic coasters featuring the quaint cottages, and what I thought was a German newspaper (although upon closer inspection, it turned out to be Greek). Oops!

After shopping, we enjoyed delicious meats on a bun. I could not believe their mouth-watering selection of beef, pork, chicken, and sausage within their deli-style restaurants. The glass case was overflowing with choices. Chad decided to feast on a beef burger, while I chose to savor a sizable pork link. Scrumptious food! Spices within the sausage enhanced its natural robust flavor. I love herbs and garlic. You cannot get such food in America. The fresh cuts were so much tastier than the processed and packaged sausage dogs available in the States. Theirs were succulent, tender, and flavorful. Desiring meat at every meal may be another German preference that I acquired from an early age.

Only hours after eating, we were catching another train back to the airport. I doubted that I would encounter another helpful man like the one who had directed us onto the correct platform. As I paced worriedly beside the railway, I discovered a German woman devouring a roasted pork sandwich. I greeted her

"German Meats on Buns"

as politely as possible, hoping that she might provide some assistance. I could tell that she didn't want anything to do with me.

"Is this the train back to Frankfurt airport?" I questioned her.

"Yes," she confirmed, looking me twice over.

"Thank you," I smiled. Since she seemed to be proficient in English, I decided to try and make conversation with her. "This is my first time in Germany," I ventured. She didn't seem interested. "My ancestors came from Germany many years ago, and it's a special place for me to visit." I watched as her attention peaked.

"Oh, really?" she questioned, with a turn of her head. She locked her gaze upon me and held it there. I felt as though she were evaluating me, inspecting me, perhaps, to see if I could possibly be from German blood.

"Yes," I elaborated, "it was my great-great-great grandfather who brought my family from Germany to America." I could tell that she was accepting my story as truth. "The language was lost," I admitted. "It's a shame."

"Yes," she jumped into the conversation. "There are people that I know who have moved out of Germany, and they have completely lost the language in a few generations. They can't speak it at all!"

"Well, that's the same with me," I confessed. "I lost that piece of my heritage."

She looked at me sympathetically now, as if I were her poor disabled German sister. For the first time, I could tell that she recognized me as a person. Briefly, she gave me a faint smile. I was a fellow German, even if I were several generations removed. Her shift in attitude was remarkable. She spoke with me until my train arrived and then bid me farewell.

On the ride back to the airport, I pondered my day. I could not believe that I had acquired so much knowledge in so little time. After less than a day in Germany, I had learned many things about this polished little country, with its highly focused and efficient citizens. But mostly, I had taken a deeper look at myself. Overall, I liked what I saw. I was hard-working, independent, and capable. But there were a few glaring rough patches in my personality that needed smoothing. By interacting with others that were a bit too much like myself, I decided that I should make a conscious effort to be more patient, compassionate, and helpful. These were the qualities that I had greatly appreciated in a few of the Germans I had met. At the end of the day, I was grateful to have experienced the German culture. My encounter had helped me explain a lot of things about my past, in addition to gaining a better understanding of who I was at the present. But most importantly, the experience had encouraged me to plan for being a better person in the future.

I was going to make an earnest effort to assist others whenever possible, and try to genuinely understand their situations. All this from only the first day of my journey! I was eager to discover what else I could learn while abroad. This was going to be a tremendously insightful adventure.

After delving into my family heritage and investigating aspects of my personal culture, it was time to nurture my inner artist. I was bound for Italy. Lovely Italy. Oh, the things I would come to cherish in Venice, Tuscany, and Rome . . . .

"Canal in Venice"

THE MASTERPIECE OF VENICE

There are many types of art: visual, musical, culinary, and architectural. You can find all these in Venice. As an artist and a teacher of the visual arts, I simply adore this city. The landscape is a piecemeal of 118 islands, separated by 150 canals, and connected by over 400 bridges. There is no other place like it in the world.

Still, I wouldn't call Venice beautiful. She's really not. Her age is much too apparent. Time-worn buildings are crumbling into murky green waters like wrinkled skin folding over varicose veins. She's less attractive than intriguing. Her alluring charm is what makes Venice so appealing. It gives her a sense of power that mere beauty would not. There are many words that could be used to emphasize her character. Unique, majestic, dramatic, and bold are a few descriptors that hint to the city's all-encompassing essence. Entering this realm is like crossing into a new dimension. Venice has a definite aura. She has the vibrancy and spunk of a teenager, coupled with the experience and wisdom of Methuselah.

I was entranced by the city from the moment that I entered, as though the air were filled with the tune of a charmer's flute-like pungi. The streets were strangely vacant in early morning. Walking through the narrow passages, I became captivated, swaying back and forth along the uneven cobblestones. Was I digesting Venice or was Venice ingesting me? It felt like a little of

"Buildings with Linins and Flower Boxes"

both. I was caught within her winding intestinal passageways. Each turn in the unpredictable maze lead to another unknown alley or abrupt dead end. I could lose myself here—spend a lifetime and not uncover every nook of the city. There was a fervent curiosity in knowing what lay around each corner. Maybe around the next bend there would be an over-sized arched doorway protected by scrolled iron-work, awaiting my appreciation. The thought of stumbling upon a stone fountain, trickling with cool water, was a refreshing possibility. Perhaps there would be another marble statue tucked away to reward a diligent explorer. The possibilities kept me rambling through her twisted belly.

Deteriorating dwellings soared stories above me, adorned with balconies of blooming flowers and drying white linens. These vertical walls provided an unmatched sense of privacy in a city so tightly packed with structures. Deep gashes in the smooth plaster faces revealed decades of repairs. Red bricks protruded through eroded scars. Each building was like a well-planned artwork. Mesmerized by one of these architectural sculptures, I noted every detail: the way the blue-green paint contrasted with the warm hues of the brick, the texture differences between the slick stucco and the porous mortar, and the balance of the ideally-spaced chips in the façade. It all seemed so perfect—too precise. The atmosphere was surreal. No actual place could have such a created feel. It was overly artistic! I felt as though I were standing on a

"Hidden Statue"

giant movie set. Every detail seemed to be thoughtfully fashioned—more like props than an authentic space. Outdoor tables with wicker chairs dotted the sides of the main canal. Arched bridges crisscrossed in every direction. Slender church steeples stretched toward the sky, amid massive domed roofs. Colorful boats bobbed rhythmically in the waters, as they tugged gently on the ropes that held them to piers and wooden piles. The scene surrounding me could have been birthed from a Bellini painting. Lovely tiled roofs, tall sporadic chimneys, and slim shuttered windows were all prominent features in my view. Venice was a great theatrical backdrop, and I was now a character in her story. I felt so alive!

These man-made aquatic surroundings were exquisitely unique. I admired the sleek ebony gondolas, with their distinctly curved ends, cruising down the waterways. They were such handsome boats. The long, narrow vessels were once a primary means of transportation for nobility. Now, they served as a symbol of the city, one that was rich in Venetian tradition. The art of making these stealthy sliders has been around since at least the ninth century. Prior to visiting Venice, I had only read about the process.

Apparently, an authentic gondola is hand-crafted from 280 pieces of oak, fir, cherry, walnut, elm, mahogany, larch, and linden. Because each wood retains certain properties, it must be used for a specific purpose. The solid oak, for instance, is crafted for the sides of the vessel, while the lightweight fir is selected for the flat bottom. Walnut and elm are both flexible and used in fashioning the frame. Cherry is easily shaped, so it is made into the thwarts. Linden is used because of its stability, and larch is desirable because it is lightweight, solid, and water resistant. Some of these woods must be curved through a process of soaking in water and heating with fire. There is so much attention to detail in constructing a gondola. Eventually, the boat is even custom aligned to accommodate the weight of its owner, so that it glides parallel to the water. Every part of the creation is well-planned and functional. The gondolier's lengthy beech-wood oar pivots on the forcola to propel the boat forward, turn left and right, or move backwards.

Many gondoliers further embellish their boats with decorative ironwork on the front and intricate golden woodwork along the sides and interior. The seats are often free-standing lushly upholstered chairs. It takes around three months to complete a gondola. The time and expense involved in its creation may account for the hefty price of $25,000 and upward.

The cost for a forty-minute ride in a gondola is no less jaw dropping. Typically, the best rate is just over a hundred dollars, but expect to pay more at night or during peak seasons. Thus, these time-honored crafts are currently reserved for leisurely tourist rides, while actual transportation is being replaced with more economical—although less elegant—public motorboats.

I rode the ferry many times down the main canal for a reasonable fee. It was noisy, offered minimal seating, and was filled beyond capacity. Nevertheless, it transported tourists and locals alike from one point to another. I did observe, however, that most residents preferred their own boats or maneuvering by foot over the numerous bridges to get from place to place within the city.

In general, Venetians didn't seem fond of tourists. I was intently ignored—possibly even snubbed—on more than one occasion by suit-clad businessmen toting briefcases. My attempt at Italian didn't earn so much as a head turn. I tried to envision things from their perspective. It would be annoying to have your city flooded daily by a sea of new, foreign faces. I'm not sure that I could be any more accepting of such a phenomenon in my own hometown. Hence, I shrugged off any animosity that came my way and concentrated on absorbing as much of Venice as possible.

Anyone relying on tourism, on the other hand, was remarkably receptive. The gondoliers were especially friendly, and easy to spot. Loitering near their boats, they were dressed in black-and-white-striped shirts, coordinating black pants, and straw hats that dangled with streaming red ribbons. They looked as if they had been waxed with a fresh coat of machismo in order to

"Gondolier"

match their highly veneered vessels. Big grins, projected chests, and open-hand gestures advertised their availability.

"Would you like to go for a tour?" a dark-haired Italian offered, as he stepped aside to reveal his prized possession.

I peered over the rails to inspect his slim glossy ride. It was much more impressive in person than literature alone could have conveyed. "Maybe," I tried to sound reluctant, not wanting him to know that I simply had to cruise in a gondola before leaving the city.

"You are my first customers, so I will give you the best deal of the day," he continued his sales pitch. "I will take you up a side canal and down the main canal for only €60."

From my research, I knew that this was a good price. I was exceptionally tempted, but my cautious husband was reluctant to accept, before surveying other options. I could tell that the gondolier was insulted. Of course, he perceived a spin in his well-groomed treasure to be worth more than twice this amount. "Well . . .," I stuttered.

"Come on, this is student rate," he protested.

I nudged Chad to the side and tried to have a private conversation with him, but there wasn't much I could do about the eavesdropping gondola man. "I really want to do this," I pleaded my case. I could tell that he really *didn't* want to do this, or at least he had no desire at that moment. I knew I could win him over, if I persisted. "I read that it is best to take the rides early in the day because they only become more expensive the later it gets." In my peripheral vision, I could see the red-ribboned straw hat nodding in approval of my rationale. The gondolier began to relax, aware now that I had done my research concerning the operation of Venetian gondolas. Chad must have realized both the logic and longing in my voice. Ultimately, he gave in.

I am so glad that he did! It turned out to be the most romantic experience since our wedding day. Don't get me wrong. I'm not usually a sucker for fairytale romance, but this really was magical. The gondolier escorted us into his boat as if we were royalty, sitting us down upon a cushy miniature loveseat. Chad wrapped his arm around me, and I snuggled into his chest. I felt so happy, so loved. With a push against the stairway and a stroke of his oar, the gondolier sent us slowly floating down the canal. I closed my eyes and listened to the sounds of Venice. It was so peaceful here in the morning. The water splashed beneath the oar, trickling from the paddle into the canal before being submerged again with a plop. Plunge, drip, splish. The sounds were so calming. From side to side, the boat gently swayed with each row. I felt as though I were being rocked to sleep with a lullaby of pleasant rain. I listened drowsily, feeling my every muscle loosen. Peace caressed me. I relaxed for what seemed like hours, although I know that it was only minutes.

DONG, CLANG, BONG! I sat straight up and jolted to attention. The church bells were striking ten o'clock. Oh, how beautiful they were! Each tower emitted its own melody within the synchronized orchestra. Many of the tones were loud and deep, as they echoed through the city. A few were tinny, and others were eloquent. The repetitive chiming blended into a distinctive Venetian symphony. I felt like the music was calling me somewhere—drawing me into Venetian life. The sound gradually dissipated after each strike. Ding, clank, pinnggg. At last, the reverberations softly mingled and faded into the distance. The silence was haunting. Already, I missed the ringing bells.

We entered the main canal, and the hush was replaced with a conglomeration of sounds: the bustle of chatty tourists, the roar of speedboat engines, and the singing of gondola operators. How I loved to hear the booming Italian voices.

"Ti voglio bene . . . ," thrust its way into the air, over the lips of the Italian serenaders, and into the souls of all who could hear. The romance was so thick that I couldn't help but breathe it in. At that moment, I had everything. I was young and in love, drifting through the canals of Venice with my best friend in celebration of our past decade together. This was exactly where I wanted to be. I inhaled deeply and tried to take a mental snapshot of the moment. This is one of my fondest life memories. I realized it then, and I know it now. I will never forget our gondola ride in Venice. It was MAGNIFICO!

All too soon, the storybook encounter came to an end. The Venetian clock struck midnight, so to speak, on this Cinderella story. We had returned to the starting point, and it was time to exit the boat. The gondolier helped us from our throne-like perch, and we returned to our humble existence.

Our enchanting gondola ride had consumed most of our allotted spending money for the day, so Chad and I made our way to a private spot where we could enjoy our rations. We had brought roasted peanuts, dried cherries, and beef jerky from home. The weakened dollar against the rising Euro had made such provisions a necessity. My German planning and Chad's packing abilities had ensured that we would not go hungry; we had enough food for three weeks. Through the winding side streets, we found a secluded spot at the edge of the city. It was spectacular. The wind-pricked ocean spread out before us in thousands of cresting peaks. In the distance, we could see a mainland bridge of Italy, serving as a lifeline, the way an umbilical cord connects an infant to its mother. Gulls flew overhead between the landmasses, shrieking and squawking. The green canal waters blended with the turquoise sea, creating a vivid aquamarine. Boats skidded across the brilliant blue bay like dazzling white skipping stones. Their wake rippled out, and surges of water lapped against the concrete support-wall beneath us. We sat there on the fringe of the city, passing our peanuts and jerky, while we absorbed the sights and sounds of Venice. It was nice to find our own small piece of the island.

Our lovely seclusion was bound to dissipate through some type of intrusion. I just never expected it to be interrupted by aviary guests. Within minutes, a crew of curious, uninvited pigeons came waddling out to greet us, cocking their heads upward and bobbing their necks back and forth in rhythm to their strides. "So nice that you could come and visit," they seemed to welcome us. "Mi casa is su casa," they hesitated, and shuffled a little closer. Our new friends didn't seem to mind what language we spoke or that we planned only to spend the day, as long as we shared our lunch with them. I watched them flap their wings and dance around on their toes. They were trying their best to be polite in their obvious request for food. We couldn't resist the entertainment of feeding them.

Their group dynamic reminded me of the three stooges. There was a bossy Moe, a fumbling Curly, and a bullied Larry. We spent over an hour dividing a handful of peanuts and hurling them into the fluttering mob. The more we fed them, the bigger the flock grew. All the pigeons in the area wanted in on the action. It was comical watching the crowd make a mad dash for the coveted prize. The faster they walked, the more rapidly their heads

"Moe, Curley, and Larry"

bobbed, as if the motion of their legs was winding a spring in their necks. They appeared mechanical. Scampering more quickly sent their tiny heads nodding, until a flap of the wings could slow them down. Waddle, bob, flap. Hilarious! Laughter bubbled out of me at their performance.

I tried to reward every pigeon with at least one treat, but the survival of the fittest was evident. One poor fellow was the slowest and scrawniest. He was the little Larry of the group. Chad and I tried, time and again, to land a nut at his feet, but he couldn't seem to grab it before another bird would seize the food and gobbled it down. We hit him square in the head with a couple, but it was no use. Moe would swoop in and steal it every time. Finally, the unfortunate guy managed to nab a bite. This outraged the boss bird so much that he started pecking Larry and pulling out his feathers. That's when we decided to leave and take our peanuts with us. We weren't going to be hit instigators within the Italian pigeon mob. It was time to return to human society.

By noon, the quiet Venetian morning was lost to an ocean of noisy day tourists. We returned to the interior of the city, barely able to walk down the overcrowded central street, which ran parallel to the main canal in sporadic walkways that occasionally ended at the side of a building. The place was packed. Close proximity to so many other perspiring bodies somehow intensified the rays of the scorching sun. We decided to investigate a few of the many Venetian shops in order to escape the sweltering heat.

The cool air inside the boutiques was almost as delightful as the displayed collection of merchandise. Decorated carnival masks came in every size and design. They were Mardi Gras in style and made from painted papier-mâché, porcelain, or stiffened fabric. Jester hats, musical notes, jewels, feathers, and elaborate face embellishments adorned each faux face. Apparently, it had been popular during the thirteenth century to disguise one's identity, while participating in risqué behaviors. This usage, along with the influence of theatrical comedy, had produced an array of these elaborate face coverings, which were now reserved for festivities surrounding Carnevale's Fat Tuesday.

Although intriguing, the masks did not fascinate me as much as the spectrum of Venetian glassware. The hand-blown artworks that lined the walls, tables, and all available surfaces were breathtaking. With the sun shimmering through each translucent form, it was like looking into a rainbow. Greens, blues, reds, purples, oranges, and yellows, glinted in multifaceted designs. Some of the glassworks were fashioned into jewelry; other pieces were made into intricate sculptures. The largest creations were stunningly symmetrical vases.

Because I had blown glass for a semester at the Art Academy of Cincinnati, I truly appreciated the skill and time

"Venetian Glass"

involved in manufacturing such works. My instructor had studied over fourteen years, being trained by three different master craftsmen, in order to produce his delicately thin goblets. Practicing the trade for only a few months, you can imagine the thick, lopsided forms that I managed to output. Absolute paperweights!

Flashbacks of the glass studio burst into my consciousness. A furnace, filled with molten glass, baked the air until the stale gasses became suffocating. Still, students didn't seem to mind. As long as we could continue our work, we were content. We were driven. Glowing orange blowpipes twirled like marching batons in and out of cylindrical, white-hot glory holes. The surroundings were concrete-gray except for these blazing-orange bubbles, which inflated slowly after each laborious breath. Artists, sweaty and dehydrated, rushed to their benches, sculpting the cooling glass with dampened wooden blocks that resembled old-fashioned soup ladles. I could smell the smoking cherry wood that was inevitably singed by the fiery glass. The calipers stopped shaping, as the transparent material hardened. Clink, clank, the metal tongs slipped over the slick exterior.

"Be sure to flash before adding color," I heard my mentor shout above the roar of our inferno. I heeded his advice. Then, I rolled the burning mass of glass uniformly over the marver's flat, silvery surface. The fragments of reds and blues melted into the

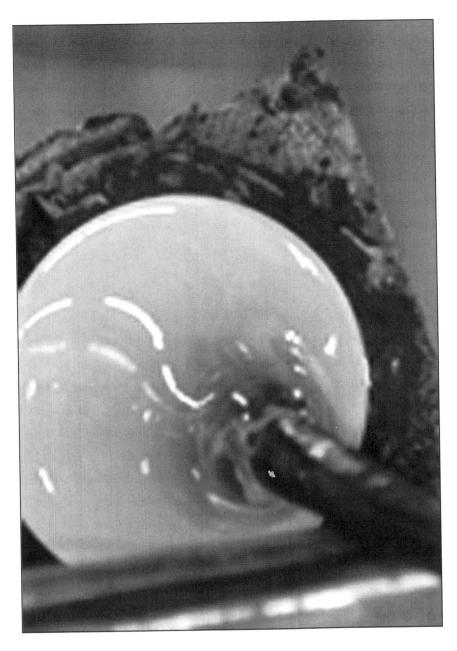

"Hot Glass on Blowpipe"

bright surface, intermingling for a streak or two of purple. I paused to appreciate the beauty. All around everyone was flashing habitually, working hurriedly, and rotating constantly! How many hours had it been? My form was finally finished, and it was time to score a jack line. Round and round to make the grove, I tried to keep it even. Tap SHARPLY, catch with gloves, and rush the piece into an annealing oven. I prayed it wouldn't shatter. Oh, the madness, the repetitiveness, the rapid pace of this tiring scramble—the race to form glass continued to invigorate my soul.

Looking around the glass store, I didn't see earrings, ornaments, or figurines. I saw the aching muscles, the glistening foreheads, and the feverish determination of the gaffers. I was infected by the same illness that had plagued them since the eighth century—a compulsion to create. Without warning, I had to own a sample of this fine Venetian history. My eyes scanned over the available selection. One pendant stood out among the rest. It was an organic leaf with gold and silver gilding that sparkled upon an emerald background. I strung the black leather cord around my neck, clasped it, and determined that it must be mine. Luckily, Visa was on my side, and I exited the shop wearing my glimmering treasure.

Outside, I smacked into a wall of heat. Since I couldn't afford any more glass shopping, I desperately needed another way to cool off. Perhaps a chill from the inside out would do the trick.

Ice cream sounded good, but I discovered that they didn't serve this American specialty in Italy. Instead, they offered something better. Gelato! Italians have been enjoying this frozen treat since the sixteenth century when Bernardo Buontalenti graced the court of Catherina dei Medici with this tasty invention. Gelato comes in all flavors, and like many gourmet ice creams, it is denser, less airy, and contains a low percentage of butterfat. This specific composition results in a more flavor-filled blend.

I ogled the vast selection of possibilities: chocolate, vanilla, and fruit mixes were especially appealing. Eventually, I opted for coconut. Heavenly! The texture was tantalizingly creamy. The bits of coconut were sweet and flaky. On the verge of being frozen, the gelato immediately melted in my mouth, coating every taste bud with cool satisfaction. As soon as I had finished my first cone, I was ready to devour another one. Next was chocolate. Lavishly decadent! Every lick was brimming with rich cocoa. The scoop was pleasantly silky against my tongue. I polished off this second serving, only to crave more. Chad's choice was cherries and cream. I took a bite. The slightly tart cherries were calmed by a lusciously smooth dairy splash. Glorious! This was so much better than the grainy, sugary ice cream from home. I was certainly going to miss gelato once I left Italy. On my mental list of favorite foreign foods, I recorded this special soft serve— right under Chinese breakfast bao and Brazilian fruit juice.

"Chad Eating Gelato"

There were still parts of the city left to explore, so after our sizable snack, we set out to find them. We managed to stumble upon Marco Polo's house—or so we were told—although it didn't look any more special than the other ancient multi-storied buildings. Also, we visited St. Mark's square, which is the nucleus of Venice and supposedly the most photographed plaza in Europe. Crops of yellow parasols sprouted up to shade swank café tables. There were so many hidden surprises tucked away in Venice. The most unique area I found nestled into the city was the Jewish Ghetto. As one of the less traveled districts, Chad and I found an escape from the tourist invasion, which had been pouring from the train station all afternoon. A tranquil stroll through the inviting neighborhood provided a glimpse into an extensive history.

Even though the surroundings looked basically the same as anywhere else in Venice, there was a different atmosphere in the Jewish Ghetto. It is difficult to explain. The buildings looked basically the same, each several stories high, lined with skinny windows, and adorned with lots of arches. Nearby, canals still hummed with traffic. Conversations were being conducted in Italian. Yet, the Ghetto felt completely secluded from the rest of Venice. I believe this sense of alienation has a lot to do with its history.

In 1516, the Venetian Republic segregated the Jews by obligating them to live at the site of the ancient foundries (campo gheto), which is where the term "Ghetto" originated. Jews were confined to this Ghetto from sundown to dawn. After curfew, the gates were locked and guards stood watch at the entrances. Members of the community were required to wear identifying badges. They could only work at permitted professions, including physician, lender, and merchant. Residents could rent, but not own property. Although limiting, the Ghetto did offer Jews safety at a time when many European countries were expelling non-Christians. Inside the protective walls, Jews were able to worship freely within their synagogues. This lifestyle lasted over 280 years, finally coming to an end when Napoleon conquered the city in 1797. With this transition of power, the gates were demolished and Jews were allowed to settle other areas of the city. Nevertheless, they were not granted full citizenship rights until 1818. While the separation of the Ghetto from the rest of Venice was dramatic during the sixteenth through eighteenth centuries, a subtle aloofness can still be felt today.

There is no mistaking being inside the Ghetto. A small distinct opening marks its entrance, and an engraved stone reads "Gheto Vechio." Some men wear black scull caps, dark clothing, and two lengthy braids. Many women cover their heads and wear long, neutral-colored dresses. The atmosphere is calmer and more orderly than outside the walls. Restaurants and markets may be marked as kosher, if they sell items following Judaic law.

"Ghetto Entrance"

Although my clothing and lifestyle were obviously not aligned with Judaism, no one stared at me or made me feel unwelcome.

I sat peacefully in their public square and contemplated the world's three great religions: Judaism, Christianity, and Islam. Why couldn't these people coexist harmoniously? The Christians had killed hundreds of thousands in their ancient crusades; the Muslims were inflicting similar destruction through terrorism, and it seemed like everyone had always wanted to annihilate the Jews. Why? Amid the tranquility of the Venetian Ghetto, tolerance seemed so simple. I could wear my shorts and eat my non-kosher jerky, and the Jewish people could wear their head coverings and buy their specially prepared meats and cheeses without either of us getting bent out of shape about it. I couldn't understand why everyone didn't accept such differences.

It wouldn't bother me if someone prayed five times a day toward Mecca, ate the body of Christ for communion, or transferred their sins to a chicken before slaughtering it for the poor during Kaparot—as long as no one was hurt in the process. Unfortunately, people often let diversity bother them. Perhaps they are scared of the unknown, or maybe within their narrow-mindedness, differences are interpreted as inferiorities. For whatever reason, religion—an institution designed to bring out the best in humankind—has perpetuated more death and atrocity than any other factor. How? Alas, I was never going to wrap my mind around it. I decided to save further spiritual contemplation for my time in Israel, which was still several days away. While in Italy, I was going to focus on stirring my artistic core.

The impact that Venice had already had on me made it difficult to pull myself away from the city. I felt sad to leave. There was so much to appreciate in one small spot. I had been captivated by the music, awed by the master craftsmen, and rejuvenated by the genius of gelato. Yet, nothing compared to the masterpiece of Venice herself. She flaunted a unique charm, dignified class, and steadfast endurance beyond all others. I learned a lot from her example. Beauty wasn't as important as character when it came to attractiveness. Venice, with all her cosmetic flaws, was irresistible. I would never forget her timeworn features, her romance, or the way her colors reflected within the picturesque canals like windows into her soul. She was timeless. I had met a friend in Venice whom I would never forget, but whom I would probably never see again. The moment was bittersweet. At the time, thoughts of gorgeous Tuscany lessened the sorrow of leaving Venice behind. I focused on possible adventures that lay ahead. What did Tuscany have in store for me?

I'm glad that I hadn't known. If I had realized then what I know now, I would not have been comforted by thoughts of rolling hills. For me, there would be few pleasantries under the broiling

Tuscan sun. But one thing was for sure, I would never forget my unusual experience.

UNDER THE TUSCAN STRAIN

At last, we had arrived in Tuscany. This was the land of enchanting movie romance, rolling picturesque vineyards, and wispy cypress trees. Optimism and happiness were invincible here. Weren't they? I bolted out of the train station ready for a passionately windswept afternoon. If I *had* been starring in a movie, this would have been the scene where half-a-dozen cameras panned their way around my swelling bosoms and came to focus on my magnanimous smile and fluttering golden strands. Momentarily frozen in time, I fondly anticipated a blissful afternoon drive.

The rental car facility was directly across the street, just as the internet blog had described. I practically floated inside, but my bubble was quickly burst. The company was no longer operating under the Hertz franchise. I felt my expectations deflating. We did not have a rental arrangement with this new agency. To make matters worse, the new Hertz office down the street had not yet opened, and it was obvious that the people in the established office were bitter against their competition. The owner was quick to warn me that the monstrous Hertz company would try to charge my credit card under the cancellation policy. Worried sigh. But she didn't stop there. She went on and on about how terrible they had been to work with. Did you know that they make it a point to cheat their customers? I was unaware of this, but she would have sworn it on her mother's grave. Furthermore, according to her, you cannot contact them because you are bounced around the departments before being placed on infinite hold. There was no limit to her distaste for the company. Anyone could see that they were a conniving, money-hungry corporate beast. She despised Hertz. If she hadn't been so serious, she wouldn't have been nearly as entertaining. Given the opportunity to rid the world of a single evil, she would surely have annihilated Hertz. In all my Tuscan travel books, no one had mentioned the anti-Hertz establishment in Chiusi with the brown-haired rental Nazi. How could all the guides have omitted this? The office was rapidly becoming a prominent figure on my Tuscan postcard.

On the brighter side, the rental commander behind the counter was also assuring us that she could provide us the same type of car at the quoted price. We accepted her offer, after a short excursion to photograph the securely locked Hertz building.

"It was a really good idea for you to take those pictures," the rental chief complemented us upon our return. "That way, you can prove that they shouldn't bill you." She would have supported anything that would stick it to Hertz.

In reality, though, I think that she was a bit nervous to have such a legally-minded customer. Americans, in general, were sue-crazed. If college had taught me nothing else, I had learned to

"Empty, Locked Office"

collect lots of evidence in case of a courtroom battle. She continued to slander the Hertz name and started going on about how much more upstanding and superior her business was. This part really made Chad nervous. He thought she was full of it. Why was she trying so hard to convince us that she was honest? Her behavior probably should have made me more fretful than it did. At the time, I just assumed that bragging on herself was a natural aspect of further degrading Hertz.

Prior to turning us over to Geraldo—that's just what I call him because of his uncanny resemblance—she gave us her cell phone number in case anything should happen. If anything *should happen*? This really should have been when my mental warning sirens began wailing. In the movies, the scene would have been played out with tense music and the camera freezing on the scribbled phone number. You might even catch a glimpse of a diabolical smirk on her lips. Unfortunately, I didn't get any such wonderful clues in real life. There was only this uneasy feeling. It was certainly strange for her to provide us with her personal cell number.

We left the office and walked around to the back. I watched Geraldo roll our itty-bitty European vehicle down from a car lift, drive out of the garage, and position it in the middle of the gravel parking lot. It was bright blue, extra small, and quite rounded, resembling a giant bird's egg on wheels. Geraldo and I pranced around the blue oval, as he led the rehearsed waltz, pointing out every dent or scratch that was marked on his scale drawing.

"The car must be returned in this same condition," he warned. The seriousness in his face was matched, and then doubled, by the intensity of my return gaze. I had no desire to repair any cosmetic flaws on their scratched and dented rental egg. Suddenly, I was the one pointing out the body blemishes and checking his diagram. I was coming to the conclusion that Rental-Nazi and Geraldo were quite the pair. Perhaps I had less to worry about with Hertz! When some of my noted imperfections were "too small" to record, I started snapping photos to add to my collection of evidence. I circled the car about five more times, photographing every square inch of its surface. Finally, I felt confident that I could win my anticipated legal suit. He seemed sufficiently unnerved by my picture-taking frenzy—enough to think twice before charging me for false damages. (Or at least, I hoped.)

Chad and I were exiting the parking lot when the clutch stuck for the first time. "This thing is a little hard to shift," he complained. Unfortunately, we both dismissed the inconvenience and set out on our journey around Tuscany. We would later come to regret this decision.

"Tuscan Scenery"

The afternoon began, as a relaxing day in Tuscany should, with gentle breezes, breathtaking scenery, and plenty of golden sunshine. I was especially admiring the rolling landscape. The curves of the Earth were gracefully sensual, as if Mother Nature were a voluptuous woman, reclining to form the hills. Fields of yellow wildflowers cloaked the ground and reflected warm sunbeams back toward the royal blue sky. Lush vineyards wound through the valleys, with symmetrical rows of twisting vines and spherical clusters. This picturesque wine country was every bit as gorgeous as impressionistic paintings. Rows of towering cypress trees lined up to salute the surrounding beauty. Their repeating vertical silhouettes created a delightful visual rhythm. Lovely bouquets of daisies, vetch, and poppies grew in clusters of oranges, violets, and reds as natural gifts to passersby. I felt welcomed by this place. And it was ours for the day. All ours. The flowing terrain was dotted with quaint tile-roofed houses, and there were no other people in sight. Chad pulled the car over every few feet, and I hopped out to capture the scene.

Click, snap, clack. My camera recorded the moment. I framed photo after photo through the viewfinder, edging my landscapes with the height of a cypress tree, ensuring that blurred wildflowers were visible in the foreground, and off-centering a cottage or a hay bale as the focal point. Each time I climbed back into the car, I noticed that it was more difficult for Chad to shift gears and accelerate. At first, neither of us commented on the issue. We were probably hoping that the problem would resolve itself. However, the harder it became to change gears, the clearer it became that the shifting troubles were not going to dissipate. My sunny afternoon was clouding with transportation worries. We decided to head back.

Before reaching the small town of Chiusi, we stopped at a gas station for drinks. The three-dollar Cokes were the highlight of another meal of jerky and peanuts. We munched contently on our lunch, observing the Tuscan crowd of a half-dozen refueling locals. The atmosphere was much like my rural hometown: quiet, calm, and casual. I decided that the environment, even physically, resembled my hometown, although the rolling hills here were not as high or steep as those in Kentucky. Well, there were vineyards here too, instead of tobacco fields. And Vanceburg had more oaks than cypress. Also, everyone was speaking Italian, rather than English. But other than those differences, I felt quite at home. There was considerable potential for having a perfectly pleasant day. It *could* have turned out that way . . . but it didn't. Before we could get back into town, we experienced a mechanical meltdown. The car started missing. Our egg-on-wheels was hiccupping slowly down the road.

At the intersection, my automotive fears manifested. The car stalled with a pitiful knocking. Its engine palpitated, and then, suddenly, the life drained out of it completely. It died in the middle of the road. Motionless. As though the poor thing had suffered a massive heart attack, our sickly car came to rest in front of a bright red stop sign. Now what? I tried calmly to process what was happening, but the traffic marker loomed outside the windshield like a giant makeshift tombstone. Our car was dead, and we were plugging the lane with its useless corpse. I motioned frantically for the vehicles behind us to go around. My dreamy afternoon was turning into a nightmare. Italian drivers began honking and staring at the less than courteous foreigners, who were blocking the roadway with their expired rattletrap. My adrenaline began to skyrocket, as I anticipated the worst. I expected a distracted motorist to rear-end us at any moment. Thoughts of a tow bill, repair costs, and a mountain of additional fees bombarded my mind. How were we going to afford to revive this jalopy? We were so close to the rental office! I felt myself trying to will the bucket of bolts back into motion. I longed for a giant defibrillator, with enough volts to surge some life into the broken shell.

Chad could start our little monster in neutral, but once the engine was operational, the transmission locked tight. Of course, it wouldn't drive in neutral. We hoped that if the engine would turn over in first gear, we would be able to cruise slowly back to the rental place. Chad disengaged the engine and turned the key while in first. Nothing. Over and over again, he tried. He attempted to start it directly from second gear. Nothing. Start it in third? No. Fourth? Not a chance. I began to worry that the vehicle would become a permanent street fixture if he continued to drain the battery. In the eternity that followed, he experimented with ways of jolting life into the Frankencar. He raced the engine, pounded the dashboard, and violently shook the steering wheel. No success.

Finally, he agreed that I could try to push, while it was running in neutral. I had never learned to drive a standard transmission. That's why Chad was driving, and I was volunteering to heave its bumper into action. My dad had told me about the clutch-popping trick, but I had never been presented with an opportunity to try it. Today would be my first attempt.

I exited the passenger's side door and took my place at the rear of the car. I didn't have time to mentally prepare for the challenge before an energetic middle-aged man jumped up from his porch and rushed to my side. Unbeknownst to me, he had been watching our entire ignition-coaxing performance for the past twenty minutes. He spoke to me in Italian, but I didn't understand a word of it.

"I'm sorry," I apologized. "I don't understand what you are saying."

He spoke more meaningless Italian.

I looked at him blankly and explained, "Our car won't start." I pointed to the car.

"Rental Car"

He smiled and uttered a few more Italian words. It was obvious that he didn't understand my English any better than I understood his Italian. I waved my hand upward, to recap the fact that I didn't know what he was communicating. He responded with more Italian. I searched his body language for any clues concerning his intentions. I was unable to interpret him.

"Well, if you'll excuse me," I pardoned myself, "I have to push this car through the intersection in order to get it going again."

He nodded at me, and I hesitated, trying to figure him out. Eventually, I gave up. I positioned my hands flatly against the bumper of the car, extended my legs, and pushed with all my might. To my surprise, the Italian man did the same and within seconds the tiny car was rolling down the road. Faster and faster we pushed the car, sprinting as swiftly as we could. Suddenly, the car broke away from our grasp, and began moving on its own.

"It worked! Get in!" I heard Chad yell from behind the wheel.

At that moment, it dawned on me that I was going to have to catch the runaway car.

"Go, Go, Go!" the man behind me seemed to chant in Italian.

I didn't have time to slow down. I ran faster than I thought my legs were capable. THUMP, THUD! My feet pounded the pavement, as I raced after the car. It was getting away! I grabbed the door handle, and I felt my body lurch, as the car yanked me forward. I stumbled. "Don't fall!" I scolded. I could envision myself tripping, slamming onto the blacktop (with my fingers still wedged through the handle), and being dragged over the rough asphalt like a grated carrot. "No, I can do this," I panted, clearing the negative images from my mind. My breaths were laborious. I could feel my heart pulsating inside my chest and hear my blood pounding within my ears. I thrust ahead with all my might, opened the door, and hurled myself into the passenger's seat. "I made it," I wheezed. I could barely talk, but I gathered enough strength to shut the door.

"Where is the rental place?" Chad demanded, as we bounded down the street.

"I don't know," I confessed, "but don't stop!" I was still trying to catch my breath. "It's not far. I know it's close." I rested my weary body against the soft seat.

Just as I was beginning to relax slightly, Chad warned, "There's a stop sign at the next intersection!"

I snapped to attention. "I don't care! DON'T stop!" I shrieked. I scanned all directions. "There's nothing coming; keep going."

We plowed through the intersection like a getaway car in a theatrical chase scene. At the next intersection, I could see that there was an oncoming vehicle.

"Speed up! You can make it," I shouted. Chad hit the gas and we darted through the cross-lanes before the other car arrived. "We did it!" I squealed. Approaching the next obstacle, I could see that another car was already stopped and ready to cross directly in front of us. "Turn right!" I instructed abruptly. Chad jerked the steering wheel, and we scooted down another street, avoiding a collision.

My heart sank when I realized that we had maneuvered onto a dead-end street. Chad eased up on the gas to give us more time to think, but neither of us could envision a solution. We coasted slowly down the hill until we came to rest in front of a very stationary building. Chad gently shifted the car into reverse. It was too late. The car coughed, sputtered, and died once again. We were back to square one. The thing would only restart in neutral. "No!" I cried. I felt terribly hopeless.

I got out of the car and prepared for another strenuous go-around. This time, there was no Italian man to help me, and it was an uphill battle. I leaned into the car, applying my weight and exerting all my strength. It wasn't budging. I dug my toes into the ground and shoved with everything I had. I felt as though my muscles, bones, and inner organs were all straining in unison to push the car ahead. Ouch! I experienced a sharp internal pain. My liver ached. The car crept forward an inch. I held it there. I was already gasping for breath. Again, I heaved. We traveled another inch. The third time I pushed, I felt my exhausted legs nearly give way. "I can't do this," I wailed, with the helplessness of someone trying to shove a two-ton elephant up a hill.

Chad jumped out to assist me. He must have detected the distress in my voice. Together, we began to trudge the stubborn mammoth up the incline. What a sight! The engine was growling, both doors swung open—resembling a pair of giant ears—and two Americans (grunting and huffing) propelled the massive creature forward from behind. It was like our docile egg had hatched into a devilish elephant. Maneuvering the brute was similar to commanding a disgruntled circus animal. She was big, awkward, and uncooperative. Low to the ground, her four supports clung to the earth and resisted our guidance. Push! Thrust! Hands pressed against its backside, we strained with all our power. The mass plodded reluctantly ahead. Harder! Faster! She was too difficult to control. To warn other vehicles, Chad pounded the horn, and the beast protested in a loud, safari trumpet. Any minute, I thoroughly expected its weight to buck backwards and crush us. I tried to restrain my imagination and distress. Onward! We inched ahead.

We were making progress. With effort, we turned the monster around and began creeping up the terrain. I stared into the empty interior, which seemed *so* odd. It was rare to encounter a moving vehicle with no one in the driver's seat. To prevent the car from veering off the road, Chad darted between the steering wheel and the bumper. He straightened the wheel, ran back to the bumper, and then he nudged her forward. Heave, dash, and adjust. We were unintentionally filling the entire street with our elephant car. When an Italian driver sped toward us, I became a little unnerved. He gave us a look of sheer annoyance, as if to suggest that we should have better control over the unwieldy devil. Chad was able to tuck the driver-side ear closed in time for the European mini-vehicle to slip by. The car slid past so closely that our fingers would have been smashed if they had been caught in between.

We finally made it to the top of the hill. Chad positioned himself in the driver's seat and was able to once again pop the clutch. I made another mad dash, and the scene played out like a recurring nightmare. He barked encouragements to run faster, while my legs flew in a blur. I finally launched myself into the seat breathless and drained, slouching in misery. The only thing worse than dreaming the same miserable situation over and over again was actually *living* the same miserable situation over and over again. I was sick of chasing down a runaway car. This was not my idea of a fun vacation activity.

Luckily, Chad turned down the correct street this time, and we could see the white walls of the rental agency glistening in the distance. The gears were growling and the engine was coughing its final breaths. Rrr, phew, rher. We were puttering our way toward the finish line in first gear. The tension in the air was of marathon proportions. We had to make it to the end of the street! Of course, it would be even better if we could casually drive the car into the gravel lot, rather than heave its lifeless shell into a final resting place. I crossed my fingers, shut my eyes, and tried to telepathically send the car all of my remaining energy. When I reopened my eyes, I discovered that Chad was manipulating the turn into the parking area. I relaxed, attempting to appear as inconspicuous as possible, in case anyone was watching our return. "Everything is fine. Just peachy," I projected. I didn't want to give the appearance that anything was even slightly wrong with the car. I knew that they would charge us for the repairs, even though we hadn't broken the clutch.

When we pulled into the empty slot by the fence, the car rolled to a halt, and the engine died on cue. Chad turned the key and removed it from the ignition. We sat there for a second, absorbing the relief. I pulled down the mirror to examine myself. I was a mess. Flushed from running, my face was an unnatural shade of bright, deep pink. Fuzzy tufts of wiry hair shot up like millions of fine corkscrews over the crown of my head. My forehead, cheeks, and nose glistened with a coating of perspiration. Three or four streams of sweat trickled from the corkscrew forest over the valleys of my temples. My mouth gaped open in gulps of panting, as I still felt deprived of oxygen. I was a disaster. There was no way I could go back into the office looking like this! I smoothed out my hair as best I could, wiped the sweat from my face, and took several slow breaths in an attempt to stop hyperventilating. There was nothing I could do about my rosy skin turning fuchsia. This would just have to be part of my new, ruffled look.

When I entered the office, the man behind he counter was obviously astonished to see me. I was a little embarrassed of my disheveled appearance and felt my fuchsia face flood with crimson.

"Back already?" he questioned.

"Yes, we only wanted to drive around and see the beautiful countryside," I admitted.

"Is the car . . . parked out back?" he stumbled dubiously. In that moment, all my suspicions about him intentionally renting us a clunker were confirmed.

"Yes," I answered simply. More peeved now than embarrassed, I maintained my blood-rich hue. He looked at me as if waiting for me to say more. I locked eyes with him and matched his anticipatory stare. There was silence. He knew that there was more to my story, and I knew that there was more to *his* story. But

I wasn't about to let him know that I knew, and he wasn't about to let me know, either. He couldn't admit that there was anything wrong with the lemon he had rented me. Certainly, I wasn't going to introduce any problems with it. The silence intensified as we waited for each other to crack.

"Did you enjoy yourself?" he probed, inspecting my tousled state.

"Yes, I got all kinds of gorgeous photos of Tuscany," I expressed in a relaxingly satisfied voice. I decided to leave the connection between a pleasant day with my husband in the rental car and my rumpled appearance to his active Italian imagination.

He smiled, "That's good. I'll go and inspect the car, and then we can finish the paperwork." I smiled back, daring him to find something wrong with it. But as he left, I felt my stomach tighten. I didn't know what to expect. Was he going to bring up the clutch? Would he find a scratch that he would swear wasn't there before? I waited nervously in the lounge, pacing, then standing, and eventually sitting. What was taking him so long? I had to get composed for his return. I leaned back in the chair, crossed my legs, and tilted my head upward to face the door. He appeared through the entryway, and I presented him with my best business-as-usual face. He didn't say anything, and I tried to hide my relief. His only inquiry was whether or not we had refueled. I suppose that we had used such a small amount of petrol that he couldn't tell. He charged me a minimal five Euro for the gasoline, and I happily signed the documents. I was grateful that the strain of Tuscany was over. It had been a day that I would never forget.

I turned from the counter with the ambition of Caesar. "To Rome!" I announced, pointing at the sky with my index finger. I could feel the amusement of the shady car renter behind me. We were off.

ROAMING TO ROME

In America, trains are not a primary means of public transportation. They carry coal, steel, and other heavy freight. Only once have I seen a midnight passenger train sneak through my hometown. It was a thrilling spectacle to behold. Smooth black cars gleamed in the darkness, with large glaring windows that separated me from hundreds of sleepy faces. I wondered where these people were going, and how many other trains like this one had slipped by, without me knowing.

Italy was altogether different in this regard. People continually spilled from public stations, and the entire country was crisscrossed with commuter tracks. Having such limited experience, you can imagine my confusion inside the massive Italian terminal. There were several levels, multiple platforms, and a multitude of trains that whizzed in every direction. Which train was mine? I had ordered my tickets via the internet. To the best of my understanding, I possessed a boarding pass and a seat assignment for every connection. Electronic boards flashed red numbers and scrolled through illuminated Italian names. I had no idea what to do, so I turned to locals for assistance.

"Excuse me, does this train go to Rome?" I questioned.

"Yes," answered one man.

"No," replied another. I felt lost.

Some people stared at me, and others sneered. It was a bad time to be an American. I finally spotted an official in uniform. "Can I take that train to Rome?" I inquired hopefully, indicating my intensions with an outstretched arm.

He inspected my tickets. "Yes, you can go there by this train," he confirmed.

I was delighted by his reply and rushed back to board an open car. As I hoisted myself through the door, I noticed a middle-aged Italian woman sitting beside the entrance. "I'm going to Rome," I smiled. She shook her head from side to side. This worried me.

"Does this train go to Rome?" I sought her consensus.

"No," she informed me.

Oh, dear! I quickly leaped from the train, as I did not want to embark on a mystery ride. I could envision myself confined onboard for hours, awakening to a final destination of Slovenia. That's all I needed! What was I going to do?

I stood motionless on the platform, obviously distressed. From out of nowhere, the uniformed man reappeared in the distance. He was screaming at me, "Get on the train! That is your train. Get on it!" I could tell by the urgency in his voice that this *was* my train and I had to get on it NOW if I wanted to take it. In front of my eyes, the automatic doors began to slowly shut. I shoved the metal hatch open again with my elbow and turned to grab my suitcase. Unfortunately, I whirled around in time to watch the door slide closed. Click. Click, click, click, echoed down the tracks, every door tightly latched in succession. I tried desperately to reopen my portal to Rome, but it wouldn't budge. It was locked! I pried on the slick steel with my fingertips. I pounded on its metallic surface with my fists. Nothing. A half-dozen Italians were shrugging on the opposite side of the glass. They had been unsuccessful in releasing the steadfast grip from inside the car. We all realized that once the door to the ark had been sealed, no one else could enter. It was useless!

I hung my head and accepted that I had missed my train, even though it was sitting right beside me. There was a hiss and then a lunge. The indifferent mechanical caravan rolled down the tracks without me. Now what? I winced at the thought of purchasing all new tickets.

"I cannot believe it left!" the uniformed man approached, slightly out of breath. "The operator is not supposed to leave when someone is boarding!" he complained.

This was news to me. I formed a glimmer of hope. Maybe if missing my train were remotely the conductor's fault, I wouldn't have to pay for another fare.

"Can you help us find a train to Rome?" I pleaded. There was a momentary hesitation, as he considered my request.

Without words, he motioned for us to follow him. He led us down a walkway and into an office filled with sour-faced women, working behind computers. In Italian, he explained our situation to the grouchiest lady, who sat behind the biggest desk. The tone of her response was less than empathetic. Our interpreter protested on our behalf. Then, other women chimed into the argument. I could tell that they didn't want to help us. The man in uniform spoke louder, gestured excitedly, and disagreed with their accusations.

"They are saying that you should not have been late," he translated. He continued to vouch for us, explaining how the doors had abruptly slammed in our faces. Reluctantly, the scowling woman collected our tickets and stapled a slip of paper to them. I was so relieved! The nice official escorted us to another platform and informed us of the connections that we needed to make in order to get to Rome.

As soon as the next train docked, we jumped hastily through the parting door, heaving our massive suitcases behind us. The leather seats in the front of the train were plush and spacious. We happily settled in for a comfortable journey. There were laptop trays, cup holders, and head cushions. I could not believe how lavish the accommodations were. The huge windows were draped with miniature curtains. Pristine two-person seats lined both sides of an expansive aisle. It took several minutes for us to realize that we were riding in business class, while holding second-class tickets. Oops! Even if the train had not already been in motion, I wouldn't have gotten off for a seating adjustment. There was no way that I was going to risk being left behind again!

On the other hand, I didn't want to be fined or kicked off for disorderly conduct. I decided to investigate second class and see if we could relocate to the proper section. A few cars back, the hallway narrowed, and private seating compartments lined the left-hand side. Not too bad. The seats were smaller and covered with cloth. I decided that this must be first class, so I kept walking. There was no questioning where second class began. The seating shrank to dwarf-size hard plastic chairs that were crowded together, filling most of the available interior. A wee corridor, less than a foot across, was obstructed by luggage, blocked by standing passengers, and overflowing with screaming children. I straddled bags, squeezed between conversations, and tried to imagine maneuvering this obstacle course, while lugging two gargantuan suitcases. It wasn't going to happen! With that realization, I turned around mid-stride and headed back toward the sanctity of business class. "Pardon me," I zigzagged through the maze of obstacles, "Excuse me."

I finally plopped down beside Chad. "The farther you walk, the more congested it gets," I declared. "It doesn't look like we're going to be moving after all." Chad didn't seem

"Train Interior"

disappointed. He reclined on his soft suede throne and started reading. I decided to take a little nap.

"Tickets please," a stewardess's voice awakened me.

I opened my eyes to see a woman's extended hand. Oh no! Where were my invalid tickets? I shook myself awake and began digging frantically through my stack of papers. "I have them somewhere," I smiled nervously. Hotel information, tourist printouts, maps . . . where were they? I was dropping papers everywhere. Receipts in the floor, airline schedules in the seats. They had to be somewhere; I just had them. There's my itinerary, but that's not what I need. Looking. Having no tickets at all must be worse than presenting incorrect ones. She stood there patiently. Ah-ha! I handed her the folded slips. She examined them, frowning as she thumbed and read.

"We missed our first train," I explained, "so they issued us new passes."

"Yes, I see that," she acknowledged, "but these are for a different section of the train."

"Oh," I began, "I tried to go back there, but I couldn't get past all the people and luggage." I knew my excuse was pitiful; still, I hoped that she wouldn't make a fuss over it.

"Mmm," she muttered, glancing down the train and imagining her own numerous rounds through the ever narrowing and increasingly blockaded passageway. She said nothing else.

She simply returned our tickets, nodded, and proceeded down the hall. I sighed with relief, but I barely had time to relax before the next stage of our train adventure began.

"I think this is where we get off," Chad informed me. He had been counting stops, as instructed by the helpful Chiusi official.

We gathered our belongings and dashed off to catch our next connection. At first, I thought I was lucky to find another train official. Upon reflection, however, I'm not so sure. Chad was positive that we needed to go to one platform, but the young man in uniform told us to go in the opposite direction. Because the last station employee had been so accommodating, I trusted the worker's advice. Bad judgment. The little twit sent us on a wild goose chase to the farthest possible track. He had to know how far away it was and that we would never reach the train in time! This must have been his fun for the day—jerking around gullible American tourists.

We ran as fast as we could, while tugging and pushing our wobbly, overstuffed suitcases through hoards of people. My heart pounded inside my chest to the point where I thought that it was going to explode. My legs grew weak and shaky. I could not breathe enough oxygen into my lungs. Halfway there, on the verge of tears, I stopped to rest. I gasped uncontrollably for air. My torso doubled over, and I rested my hands on my knees to keep from falling. I knew that I could not give up. I composed my remaining energy for the rest of the marathon, and then I jogged the final stretch. When I arrived, there was nothing but an empty track. I felt as if I had just been beaten for no good reason. I fell to the ground and began to sob.

A floor sweeper came to investigate the weeping foreigner, who had collapsed on his otherwise clean concrete. "Did this train go to Rome?" I managed to ask between my blubbering.

"No," he answered. Then, he walked over to a small paper schedule stapled to a post and pointed to an Italian word. I hoisted myself off the pavement and went to inspect this miniscule printout. Beside the track number was an unfamiliar Italian name. I realized how fortunate I was to have missed the train that went to this obscure town. I may never have found my way to Rome from there. I wiped my tears away, and asked him how to get to Rome. He moved his finger down the page to the word "Roma." By this time, Chad was standing behind me, glaring over my shoulder.

"That's the track I told you we should take!" he exclaimed. He was absolutely livid. I thanked the terminal custodian, and chased after Chad. He had already stomped several yards down the walkway.

"At least we know where to wait for the train," I tried to console him.

It was no use. His adrenalin had kicked into overdrive. His breathing was deep; his pace was deliberate, and his teeth were gritted with anger. I prayed that we didn't run into the boy who had scammed us. I was fairly certain that Chad would rip him limb from limb. Then, we would be in big trouble.

"If we ever go to war with Italy again," Chad grumbled, "I am all for it!"

His statement shocked me a little. I knew that he was tired of the Italians staring at us, sneering haughtily, and belittling us because we were Americans. This last wiseguy had gone too far— running us in the wrong direction for meanness. Now, Chad wanted to blow up the whole country. He was overreacting a bit, allowing his emotions to get the better of him. I knew that he wouldn't really support the entire nation's demise once he had calmed down. I just had to keep him away from that cruel pipsqueak, who had caused us so much trouble. The farther we walked, the more he cooled.

When we arrived at the correct terminal, I could see that the doors of the cars were already beginning to close. "NO!" I shouted, thundering toward the train. "Not again!" I wasn't going to let this one get away. Determination engulfed me. I raced toward the last car as if my life depended on it. The conductor was going to have to drag me down the tracks with him, if he set this train in motion. Whack, oomph. I threw my entire body into the narrowing crack and wedged the doors apart with my back and extended legs. The entrance widened, but I did not stop shoving until the doors fully opened. "Hand me the suitcases," I demanded. Chad threw them up, one at a time, and I hurled them onto the floor. BLAM. My bag crashed onto the train first. We were both moving with the seriousness and intensity of escaping convicts. THUD. Chad's suitcase pounded into position. I looked wildly around to see if the train was moving. Not yet.

Our commotion had captured the attention of two women in the last compartment. They rushed out to evaluate the situation and were trying to calm me down. I didn't understand a word that they said, but I could tell that they were attempting to convince me that there was plenty of time. I ignored them intently. At that moment, I feverishly distrusted Italians. I wanted to be left alone, with my husband and my luggage and my raging endorphins.

"Get in!" I commanded, afraid of being separated from Chad. I was still jamming the door with my body, in a jumping-jack stance, so Chad squeezed inside between my lifted arm and propped leg.

Being safely and completely aboard, I enjoyed a rush of tranquility, which was interrupted by the snickering of the two women. They found humor, I suppose, in a couple of overly anxious Americans, who had so desperately bounded onto a stationary train. I didn't care. I knelt over my suitcase as though it were an altar, clasped my hands together, and silently thanked God that we had successfully boarded our train to Rome. The women stopped laughing. Perhaps the devout Catholics didn't want to appear less pious than the goofy outsider. When I opened my eyes, I noticed that they were smiling politely at me for the first time. My heavenly communication must have established that Americans were also human beings.

They quietly excused themselves, retreating down into their private seating area. We chose to enter the upper level. The grimy second-class seats were a welcomed sight. I was so tired that I collapsed beside Chad. It was hot! Years of perspiration had seeped into the discolored chairs. The floor was oily and sticky. Graffiti covered the cracked windows. Only one other man entered the empty car. I watched him effortlessly unlatch the closed door and stroll inside. Ten minutes passed before we began moving down the tracks. I guess there had been plenty of time after all. The town outside finally faded into countryside. Fields and flowers predominated, until the views eventually developed into crops of buildings once again. The cycle repeated over and over. Rural to urban and back to farmland. No one came to check our tickets. No one cared that we were there. The three of us sat silently in the car, Chad, myself, and the lone tourist, waiting for Rome to appear outside our windows.

EXPLORING THE EMPIRE

If I could have lived at any time and place—other than in America during the twenty-first century, with all of our current technologies—I would have been born in Italy during the reign of the Roman Empire. These people were ahead of their time. Great ingenuity within an astounding culture birthed a standard of living that would remain unmatched for over a thousand years. The Romans were fierce warriors, but they also appreciated art, relaxation, and entertainment.

For recreation, I would have fancied watching blood-tingling chariot races, with armored drivers dashing in front of one another to perpetuate spectacular crashes. Now that's a show! Charioteers hanging on for dear life, rounding hairpin turns, and occasionally being dragged for yards until they cut themselves free from the horses' reins. Wow!

Modern sports are so blasé by comparison. Players today chase after different sized balls to accumulate points. Not exactly edge-of-my-seat material. Put the big ball into the basket; get the little ball into the hole, or cross the line with the inflated pigskin. Ho-hum. I cannot force myself to watch such athletic performances. The way some people take these ball-chasing activities so seriously, I will never understand. NASCAR is just as boring to me. Racers drive around a paved circle several hundred times. After a couple hours, nothing has changed much. Three or four hours into the event, it's still the same 43 cars traveling around the same mile-and-a-half track. Blah. The first lap was more than I could stand. These competitions lack the charisma of racing-chariots, pulled by galloping horses. Oh, to be in ancient Rome! I can almost feel the thundering vibrations, smell the musty sweat, and hear the wooden wheels grating against the earth.

Even better were the luxurious Roman baths. Ingeniously engineered, these facilities boasted warmed marble floors, dry saunas, and heated bathing pools. This was the type of place where I could lose myself. High vaulted ceilings were adorned with colored marble panels. Walls were decorated with intricate mosaics, and the huge, well-lit spaces shimmered with watery surfaces and silvered faucets. In these beautiful surroundings, I could, no doubt, stay submerged within the soothingly steamy waters for hours, soaking and relaxing. Stress and time would dissolve away, and I would emerge rested and ready for other Roman indulgences. A dip in the cooling pool might stir my senses for a stroll through the lush, peaceful gardens. I could lounge for an hour or so among the vegetation. Or perhaps, a visit to the library would be the perfect after-bath activity. If I desired a bit more excitement, there were always jugglers or acrobats to watch. A little snack from one of the many food vendors would be a welcomed treat. When nature called, I could use one of the world's first "flushing" marble toilets, which were situated over shallowly water-filled channels to carry waste away from the city. Ah, the conveniences of ancient Rome were abounding and pleasurable. To be a Roman . . . to be a member of this magnificent empire . . . it would have been quite satisfying.

The mere gratification of being a Roman citizen would have been absolutely head swelling. The expansive empire stretched over present-day France and Spain to the west, encompassing Europe all the way to Scotland. In the opposite direction, the empirical influence advanced throughout Turkey, until it met the edges of the Middle East to engulf Syria and Palestine. Along the southern coast of the Mediterranean, the Roman territory fringed the top of the African continent. To be part of such a vast and powerful civilization would have been the source of tremendous pride.

Romans born during the height of the empire must have seen Rome as the cornerstone of Earth. The government, with its executive, legislative, and judicial branches, changed insignificantly through the generations. The Roman military— disciplined, well trained, and effectively equipped—seemed an unstoppable force. With control of the seas, their navy sailed unopposed throughout the Mediterranean. The Roman cavalry appeared no less invincible, boasting numerous advantages of stone-paved roads, supply chains, accurate maps, and a network of intelligence. Because Rome dominated and expanded their governed regions for over a thousand years, the society would have seemed everlasting, especially to any individual living at the time. It would have been unimaginable, then, to consider a fall from such greatness. Rome was a powerful force that was leading in ancient technological advancements. Their skilled builders were creating bridges and aqueducts which were so well constructed that they would still be standing over 2,000 years later!

I surveyed the lengthy aqueducts, uneven cobblestone streets, and abundance of rhythmic arches, marveling at Roman ingenuity. The city was built firmly, to last. She is a city of stone. Quite possibly, Rome is the heaviest city in the world. Every structure is massive—like a city of government buildings—large in scale, dotted with windows, covered in arches, and showcasing columns, domes, and carved moldings. Assembled from oversized blocks and marble, Rome is determined to endure another millennium or two.

Compared to Venice—the ornate, promiscuous daughter of Italy—Rome is the older, dependable sister. I'm sure that you've met women like Rome. Tall, big boned, and strong as an ox. She never looks quite feminine, even when her face is splashed with a fresh coat of paint and her body is bejeweled with finely carved statues. Somehow she's too bulky to be elegant. She flaunts elaborate fountains, crumbling monuments, and other splendidly-

"Buildings of Rome"

aged structures amid a modern scene, as though they were ancient buttons sewn onto a new dress. The locals pass her by, without a glance at her spectacular showcase, but the tourists come from miles away to view her collection: the Sistine Chapel, Colosseum, Trevi Fountain, and Pantheon, to name a few.

There were so many sights to see. I wish someone had warned me about how overwhelming the Sistine Chapel and its surroundings would be. Massive overhead arches grew from the marble floors of the Apostolic Palace. Semi-circular channels lined the ceilings of the hallways, which were covered with paintings and tapestries. Every square inch of the ceilings and archways was adorned with intricate artworks. The details in the Biblical frescos were glorious. Portrait subjects were so realistic that they looked as though they might step from the walls. The human forms, tinted and shaded to create three-dimensionality, were perfectly rendered as only a talented painter—who was also a master sculptor—could create. Indeed, Michelangelo was a genius. Folding robes cascaded in flowing rivulets from every direction. Oranges, yellows, and greens popped out to grab my attention, but I didn't linger. I was so concentrated on seeing *The Creation of Adam* that I rushed by many of these equally impressive artworks.

Every art textbook since my freshman year of college had featured an image of the outstretched hand of God, giving life to

Adam. To see this painting in person was almost more than I could handle. Where was it? I hoped that I hadn't overlooked the room. It would be a travesty to miss what is quite possibly Rome's most famous image. I decided to follow the crowd, and sure enough, the surge led me to the interior of the Sistine Chapel. It was like stepping inside an enormous three-dimensional painting, with artworks on all four walls and overhead.

"Silenzio," a monotone voice echoed through the narrow chapel. Three robed overseers loomed ominously from a ledge above the tightly packed crowd. One at a time, they spoke in English and Italian. "Silence, please." The low tones of their commands bounced around the small chamber of jabbering tourists.

Click, clack, click. Cameras sang. "No photo," chimed the monotone voices. There was a pause in snapping, which lasted less than a minute. Those further into the chapel began concealing their cameras and going for ninja shots, but a constant flow of fresh-faced, camera-wielding tourists poured inside. The voices alternated between their two chants: "Silence, please" and "No photo." The pulsating chatter and camera clattering dwindled and rose like the heartbeat of the interior.

I scanned the ceiling frantically. Where was it? This was the room. I was in the Sistine Chapel. Where was *The Creation of Adam*? There were lots of extravagantly cloaked scholars brushed onto the ceiling. Nude people with outstretched arms hung overhead. I recognized scenes from Genesis among the patchwork of paintings. God was dividing light from darkness and separating the water from the earth. A snake wound around a tree, and an angel banished Adam and Eve from the garden. I saw images of Noah and the great flood. Arms and legs were angled in every direction. But where was THE *masterpiece*?

Finally, I tilted my head back as far as I could and looked straight above me. There it was, near the center of the room! *The Creation of Adam* was directly above my head! A jolt of adrenaline hit me like a punch of electric. Without thinking, I instinctively grabbed my camera and snapped a picture. The resulting flash lit up the room with the intensity of a lightning strike. Oops! The monks cast stern disapproving daggers in my direction. Apparently, I had crossed the threshold of tolerance. One of the men descended his platform, and strode toward me. What was he going to do? I felt my body tense, as he worked his way through the maze of picture-snapping tourists to find the flash culprit. My grip on my camera tightened. Was he going to throw me out? Did he plan to take my camera? His scolding eyes met mine, and I smiled as innocently and apologetically as possible. I felt his warm breath on my ear as he bent forward and whispered, "Erase the picture."

"Ceiling of the Sistine Chapel"

Was he kidding? We both knew that I was not going to erase the picture of *The Creation of Adam*. This in itself felt like a sin. Destroy an image of the most recognized religious painting in all of Italy? Never! But, I decided to play along. I reluctantly consented with a less-than-convincing "okay," and then I tapped some buttons as if I were deleting something. All done. We both knew that I did not delete the photo, but there was an unspoken agreement that I was not going to take any more. He returned to his high perch, and I happily set off to see the Colosseum.

The Colosseum turned out to be my favorite attraction in Rome because it evoked the deepest emotional response. It is truly a majestic structure. The first three levels are infused with beautiful stone arches. A partial upper level gives the structure an overall asymmetrical balance that reflects its lengthy existence and provokes the imagination. I could visualize the gladiators, the animal hunts, and the battle reenactments. Its walls were simply oozing with history. Still, the atmosphere was a strange mix of excitement and pain. On the one hand, captivating matches were performed on this expansive stage. The floor had been flooded to host naval scenes. Trees and other vegetation had once been planted as backdrops for pursuing exotic game, including rhinos, hippos, elephants, lions, leopards, bears, crocodiles, and ostriches. Such massive and dangerous theatrical performances would have been dramatic to watch. It is estimated that 50,000 spectators at a

"Inside the Colosseum"

time witnessed the extermination of over a million animals and 500,000 people throughout the games. Hence, there was also a reverence here, as though the souls of thousands of slain Christians and slaughtered prisoners still lingered. I shuddered as I considered those who had been mutilated for entertainment or burned alive to light the emperor's suppers. With the wooden slats rotted away, I could peer into the cells below that had imprisoned the ill-fated captives moments before they were heinously executed. If there is such a thing as negative residual energy, it would have explained the misery and anguish that I felt wafting up from the Colosseum floor. Today, the Colosseum stands as a testament to ancient Roman ingenuity and a reminder of man's tendency toward wickedness.

I spent so long contemplating the Colosseum that we missed our last tour bus to the Trevi Fountain. Consequently, we were forced to walk across the city. I am convinced that no other place in the world mingles the ancient with the modern to the extent of Rome. Between contemporary buildings, it was not uncommon to stumble upon the remnants of an ancient structure. Other constructions seemed to defy time. Was I looking at architecture from a period closer to the 14th or the 21st century? It was difficult to tell. Almost every building appeared to be solid stone, and stone has been around forever. Like everything else in Rome, the fountain was substantial. There were so many columns,

"Trevi Fountain"

marble statues, and finely sculpted details that it was taxing to retain a proper mental image, if not directly looking at it. The water cascaded from the center of a rocky outcrop, between two rearing winged horses that were accompanied by a couple of scantily covered, muscular men. Serving as an oasis within a parched city, people washed their dusty feet at the public faucets, tourists drank and replenished their reserves from spouts, and rose peddlers dipped their bright red bouquets directly into the main pool. The smell of water saturated the area, moistening the air as it entered my lungs, and I could hear a gentle rumbling of spilling water over the boisterous crowd. Unfortunately, the space around the fountain had developed into an outdoor souvenir flea market. In addition to postcards and key chains, street merchants were attracting attention with noisemakers and firing off loud whirligigs that lit up and spun around on the sidewalk. All of this distracted considerably from the loveliness and tranquility of the fountain itself. The bustle transformed a relaxing spot into a rowdy watering hole infested with clamoring vendors. Needless to say, we soon set our sights on locating the Pantheon.

Actually finding the Pantheon felt mostly like an accident. Yes, we knew the general direction from studying our minimalist tourist map, but I never expected to practically walk right into the place. This was a classic example of ancient architecture infused within the modern city. I was rounding the corner of a café, when right in front of my nose appeared the Pantheon. It was a huge domed cylindrical building attached to a gable-roofed portico, which resembled a grandiose porch, supported by a total of sixteen towering columns. Roman residents passed by without so much as an acknowledgement, but tourists froze in admiration. By surveying the structure, I would not have guessed that it was constructed in the second century A.D. Sure, it looked old, but almost two thousand years old? This was almost inconceivable. The Pantheon had been built originally as a temple to the gods of ancient Rome. It had burned twice, before taking its current form—once after a lightning strike, which I found ironic due to its established purpose of honoring the gods. Its name had been derived from two Greek words, "pan," meaning "everything" and "teon," translated as "divine." Although it was not open for viewing when I was there, I understand that in the seventh century it was consecrated as a church and has been used as a tomb for Italian royalty and artists since the Renaissance. Some of those buried inside include painters Raphael and Annibale Carracci, composer Arcangelo Corelli, and architect Baldassare Peruzzi. The bodies of two Italian kings, Vittorio Emanuele II and Umberto I, as well as Umberto's Queen, are also among those entombed. It would have been nice to have examined the interior, but I was thankful to have had the privilege of seeing its exterior. You cannot appreciate the scale of these Roman sites, until you are

"Pantheon"

standing on the porch, so to speak. Rome is such an oversized city that I felt miniscule compared to the immensity of these surroundings.

By evening, it was time to find a smaller venue for a romantic Italian dinner. Chad and I discovered the perfect restaurant with outdoor seating. The temperature had become pleasantly cool. Nearby street lamps cast a soft golden glow over the veranda. Potted greenery surrounded the tables, and wispy ivy draped overhead. A singing violinist serenaded patrons with soul-soothing melodies. Toasty bruschetta, pink prosciutto, and meaty olives were served by a sleekly uniformed waiter. Dark hair slicked back to accent his square jaw line, our attendant was confident—like most Italian men—that he could tempt a harem with his smile. The food was attractively presented on a square milky-white plate, which reflected the vivid reds of the tomatoes and the vibrant greens in the herbs. The buttery bread was crisp with each bite, and I could discern the flavors of savory olive oil and subtly aromatic garlic. This was the best meal that I had leisurely partaken of since arriving in the country. My love of art and architecture had been satisfied by a memorable day of sightseeing, and now Italy was also filling my stomach and my heart. Only days ago, I had fallen for Venice, and now, I was succumbing to the charms of Rome. Life was good, pleasures abounded, and sleep would come easily.

"Violinist Serenades Diners"

VATICAN CITY

Where was the Vatican? We had been walking for what seemed like an eternity, and I felt as though we should have been there by now. Suddenly, I found myself halted amidst a winding cluster of people, who were all battling the scorching sun with water bottles, hats, and parasols. I stopped to take a drink. My parched tongue welcomed the wetness, but I could feel the sting of my reddening lips and taste the salt that dripped from the corners of my mouth. The slow-moving line quickly grew, snaking behind me and curving completely around the square. I had unintentionally become enveloped within this mysterious line of sightseers. Straining to see ahead, I had no idea what I was waiting to see. Women of all ages were patiently conserving their water supply by consuming small sips beneath their portable shades. Young men were guzzling fluids under protective hats. Children played water tag and poured the cool liquid over their sopping heads. The heat was blistering. My entire body was coated in a layer of glistening sweat, causing my clothes to cling uncomfortably to my torso and legs. I had been told that these lengthy garments would allow me entrance into the churches, as my knees and shoulders were covered, yet I wasn't sure that this suffocating price of admission was worth the agony. I began to wonder if this was the line to get into Vatican City.

"Is this how we get inside the Vatican?" I asked Chad. He didn't answer, so I repeated my question, "How do we get into Vatican City?"

"You are in it," an Australian man turned around to inform me.

"Oh! We are?" I questioned in surprise. "Well, when did that happen?"

He shrugged his shoulders to confess that he didn't know where the boundaries were. "Not sure," he joked, "but they speak good English over here; don't they?" I had to grin at that comment. I didn't know if he was pretending to be a resident, or if he was playing as though he thought that I was a citizen, but either way he was poking fun at my interest in crossing over into the Vatican nation.

"Yep, great English skills in this country," I laughed.

I suppose that I had been expecting a grand divide of some sort between Rome and the Vatican. I had envisioned an elaborate gate with guards that asked you about your purpose for visiting and then scrupulously inspected you, no matter what your response. I should have had to at least show my passport to someone, right? Nope. Evidently, you can walk right across the border without even realizing it. In general, this is an uncomfortable thought. Think about what it would be like if you could accidentally cross into the Congo or North Korea—the laws dramatically changing,

"Outside St. Peter's Basilica"

without your knowledge. Scary! In specific, however, going from Rome to the Vatican wasn't a big deal at all. Nothing was different. They hadn't even bothered to put up a sign. I later read that there was a white line on the ground—somewhere—that marked the boundary between the two countries, but I never saw it.

Since I was not standing in line to enter the Vatican, it dawned on me that I still didn't know what I was waiting to do. "What is this line for?" I asked the knowledgeable Aussie.

"This is for St. Peter's Basilica," he noted with an air of awe in his unmistakably down-under voice. I must not have responded with an acceptable level of excitement. "It is the biggest church in the world," he added. Still, I didn't offer the wide-eyed adoration that he was expecting. "It's worth the wait," he assured me.

He turned out to be correct. I followed the shuffling sandals ahead of me through an underground tunnel, filled with the tombs of saints and former popes. Most of the visitors began singing angelically in Latin. I didn't understand the words, but the melodic chants overflowed with praise to the extent that I felt the presence of God hug the chamber. My soul filled with love and peace. I was a part of something much greater than myself—far more powerful than human words could describe. I am not Catholic, but this didn't matter. We were not pilgrims of a single religion; we worshiped our universal creator in one accord. I felt deeply thankful to have been blessed with life; this was the ultimate gift from the Almighty.

When we arrived at the pristinely white vault of John Paul II, I observed that the lid was covered in red roses and a pile of letters had been fondly laid at his feet. The crowd was gripped with sadness. Elderly women wailed, while the young ladies and men recited scripture. I too became overcome with grief. Unexpectedly, I felt large teardrops falling from my eyes and rolling down my cheeks. I was not crying because a pope had died; instead, I was mourning the loss of a devout man. Pope or not, there was a little less good in the world without him.

After ascending a narrow, spiral staircase, the basilica opened before me like a king's palace. The sheer size of the interior was overwhelming, with an open space as big as adjoining football fields. The arch-filled ceiling was so high that it was like being inside a skyscraper with only one floor. Not only was the area expansive, it was also incredibly ornate. Gold trim outlined the ceiling, which was covered with beautifully detailed paintings. The floor was inlaid with multi-colored geometric patterns of marble. Intricately carved woodwork accented the walls, and there were frescos, mosaics, and statues everywhere. Not a bare inch could be found in the whole church. I was consumed by the lavishness of the surroundings, as if swallowed by a fairy tale. Never before had I been so impressed by a building. St. Peter's

Basilica was the Taj Mahal of the Catholic Church—a labor of love for Christianity. Apostle Peter, other saints, popes, kings, queens, and princes were buried in and under this now magnificent church. The site was a holy palace. I was rendered speechless.

Nonetheless, our encounter with the divine royal atmosphere was short lived. Upon exiting the basilica, we spent fourteen dollars on two Cokes and settled down on concrete steps to enjoy another pauper's dinner of peanuts, dried cherries, and beef jerky. I was grateful for every bite. We weren't hungry; our spirits were brimming, and the view of the basilica was excellent!

THE STONE PEOPLE OF POMPEII

On our last day in Rome, Chad and I headed to the port in Civitavecchia. We would be boarding a cruise ship that would transport us to the remainder of our destinations. It was a relief to unstrap the traveling boots and enjoy the slippers of tourism. What I mean is that there would be fewer trains to miss and more than peanuts to eat. Smooth sailing from here! (No pun intended.)

We were sailing from Italy to Italy. Okay, more specifically, we would be going from Rome to Sorrento. I wasn't that excited with the initial debarkation. As far as I knew, there wasn't anything spectacular about Sorrento. That is until . . . the cruise director told us about the stone people of Pompeii.

Apparently, Pompeii was the Las Vegas of the ancient world. It was a popular Roman vacation spot—the stomping grounds of the rich and famous. Around the sixth century B.C., the who's who of Italy felt that they had to build a house on the Strip. Er, I mean on Main Street, Pompeii. As a result, the city is filled with mosaics, frescos, pottery, functioning kitchens, and all the other fine things of the day. About 20,000 inhabitants enjoyed a food market, a bar, many restaurants, several theaters, a gymnasium, aqueducts, baths, and even a hotel. Then, in 79 A.D. the sky came crashing down on them. Mount Vesuvius blew her top and buried everything under sixty feet of ash and pumice. The

"Kitchen with Basins, Stone Walls, and Frescos"

city was abandoned and eventually forgotten. Not until the mid 1700s was the town rediscovered through excavations. Fortunately, buildings and personal belongings remained remarkably preserved, without deterioration from air and moisture, over those nearly 2,000 years. Yes, this was all fascinating, but it wasn't the most interesting part.

It was during these excavations that an archeologist by the name of Giuseppe Fiorelli started discovering empty areas within the digging sites and realized what these pockets were. He had the brilliant idea of injecting plaster into the negative spaces to recreate the forms. As a result, he was able to perfectly reproduce the poses of Pompeiian victims at the moment of their deaths. Effectively, he was filling the void left from their decomposed bodies. In many cases, their terror and anguish were evident, still etched across their faces. Wow! This was the creepiest, yet most intriguing description I had ever heard. From that movement, I *had* to see the stone people of Pompeii. Unbelievably, no one told me that you would have to hire a guide to do this!

Chad and I took a train to Pompeii. Things seemed to be going great. In fact, we had arrived so early that the place hadn't yet opened. So, we decided to take advantage of a nuclear lemon stand, where I downed the most flavorful icy of my life; it had been made from lemons the size of my head. Ahhh, I digress.

"Pottery, Columns, & Other Artifacts"

The point is that, once inside, I could not find the stone people. We walked down one cobblestone road after another. I spied the chariot tracks worn into the surfaces of the streets. I recognized the remains of houses and businesses. There were large sections of colorful and detailed frescos that decorated the walls, depicting daily Roman life. Ornate mosaics of designs, animals, and people sprawled across floors. There were massive stacks of pottery in every size and shape. Beautiful basins embellished kitchen counters. It seemed like it would have been a snazzy place to live. But, where were the remains of these former residents?

I trekked up the hills and down the slopes, peeping into every nook. No stone people. After hours of searching, I was ready to give up. There were no signs. I had no map. No one knew where they were. Some visitors, who spoke English, hadn't even heard of them. My feet were sore and blistered. My legs ached. I was about to leave the site when I heard an encouraging phrase.

"Through here are the casts of the human forms," a tour guide was informing his group.

My attention perked like the ears of a watchdog. As nonchalantly as possible, I accompanied his followers through a side entrance, which struck me as purposefully hidden. I meandered slowly through the shuffling crowd, until I caught sight of the stone people. The view was eerily alluring—a terrible moment frozen in history.

The pale statues resembled artistic sculptures. A small boy bent over his knees and clutched his nose with both hands. This posture must have been in an effort to breathe, while being trapped alive in the raining debris. His mouth was open, as if he had been screaming or crying. There was also a pregnant woman, who lay belly down, covering her face. Her form, lonely and frightened, was a testament to human loss. A dog's contorted body appeared knot-like, with its legs lunged into the air and its head hugging its backside, as though it had been strangled to death. The scene was severely grim.

The destruction of Pompeii sprung to life before my eyes. I could almost hear the people screaming, as I imagined the immobilizing fear that had gripped them during the volcanic rumbling and raining of ash. It became real to me. How could something so painful have sparked my curiosity? At some point, the stone figures had ceased to represent actual people and become merely historical artifacts. Seeing them for myself allowed my imagination to breathe life into these human forms.

I had finally found the stone people . . . and now I would never forget them. Their anguish would be forever etched into my mind.

"Stone Boy Covering His Nose"

"From Alexandria to Cairo"

PERCEIVING EGYPTIAN IMPORTANCE

"Why do we study history?" My World Civics teacher had asked me this question when I was in high school. I had never thought about the answer before that moment. It stumped me at first, so I repeated what I had been told in the past, "We study history to learn from our mistakes." He wasn't satisfied with that answer. I don't think he believed that people *did* effectively learn from previous errors. Really, I also knew that something was lacking in this logic. On a personal level, I wasn't going to be preventing a great depression or anything. Why did I study history? I struggled with this question for years after it was proposed. It took many more life experiences before I internalized the importance of history.

I remember the day that I started to form a solid answer. After teaching an art lesson on Colonial America, I imagined what it would be like to be completely ignorant of our past. How would it feel not to know where I came from, who the pilgrims were, or that slavery had once existed? It would be as though I had just been plopped onto Earth with no one living before me. I wouldn't have the mental constructs to explain religion, human rights, or existing racial tensions. Simple progress from candles to electric light bulbs would have been forgotten. I might think it merely coincidental that citizens of Britain, America, and Australia shared a common language. Imagining this scenario made me feel lost. Who was *I* in a world with no past? That was the day I understood why we study history: to learn our roots and realize our current place in the world. I am able to realize who I am and where I fit in because I have been taught about the events that occurred before me.

Based on this same reasoning, I decided to travel to Egypt in order to learn about our broader human history. Egypt's rich civilization has made valuable contributions to intellectual thought and cultural exchange throughout the millennia. Egyptian architecture, art, and beliefs have impacted us in ways that we may not even recognize. For instance, the Egyptians invented hydraulic cement, which has been adapted and used extensively in present-day construction. Indeed, many building techniques were developed during the erecting of the great pyramids, including quarrying and surveying methods. Also, their practice of mummification was a precursor of current embalming practices. No other culture, until modern times, placed such significance on preserving the body. These ancient, meticulously wrapped Egyptian corpses still captivate our imaginations. Before the global spread of the world's main religions, the Egyptians strongly believed that every human had two distinct aspects: the body and the spirit. I knew that Egypt had a long and prestigious history.

However, I was unaware of the magnitude of the Egyptian ego, until I traveled to the country and experienced it for myself.

My first up-close view of the Egyptian landscape was from a bus window in Alexandria. I could not believe what lay before me. It appeared as though the city had been built on an enormous landfill. Sporadic vacant lots were stacked with mounds of garbage, as if undeveloped areas were dump sites that remained exposed. Skyscrapers rose out of a sea of junk. Empty bottles, bags, and wrappers were tumbling and blowing down the streets in front of the high-rises. Every square foot of the city was covered in filth! I glanced around the interior of the bus to determine if anyone else was mentally choking on this scenery. Our motor coach, filled with American and Western European tourists, was completely silent, with passengers' eyes fixed outward. No one was commenting on the views. Only the voice over the loud speaker broke the tense hush.

"Alexandria is the cleanest city in all of Egypt," our tour guide, Sherry, boasted. Everyone gasped in unison. I felt the oxygen on the bus being slightly depleted during that single giant intake. I could tell everyone felt a little lightheaded. Our eyes collectively studied her in horrid wonder. "Maybe one day Cairo will be this way," she hopefully expressed. Jaws dropped open and eyebrows lifted simultaneously from one person to the next.

We could not believe what we were hearing. The group was tongue-tied. Some people shook their heads.

I looked out the window, trying to imagine it dirtier. The "Wow!" inside my head joined the other unspoken "Wows!" around the bus. She really was proud of the "cleanliness" of this city.

There were oceans of vacant desert between Alexandria and Cairo, with small islands of green randomly dotting the landscape. Sherry explained that the privately owned lands were irrigated and planted with vegetation and palm trees. The empty sands were areas that were still available. Hence, it would be easy for us to pick out a spot, if we wanted one. I didn't. It's an okay place to visit, but living there was an altogether different animal.

Another peculiar sight out my widow was an abundance of slender pillars, filled with holes. They were wider on the bottom, almost like skinny cones, but they came to a round point at the top. The lengths of the tall grayish structures were peppered with tiny openings. I could not figure out what they were. I saw one, and it piqued my curiosity. Then I spied another, and another. These things were everywhere, rising out of the earth like giant memorial stones. They were nestled between shrubs, parked beside houses, and standing defiantly in the middle of nowhere. "What are those things?" I finally asked our Egyptian leader.

She glanced out the window in the direction I was pointing. "Oh," she replied, as though this would be her easiest question all day, "those are bird houses."

I felt my eye brows squish together, rumpling my forehead. Bird houses? My mouth puckered a little, as my lips formed around the /b/ sound. Before I could repeat her response, she clarified.

"Yes," she elaborated, "they are called pigeons when they are pets, and squab when they are dinner."

I reexamined the elongated domes, armed with my new knowledge. Squab stacks. I was effectively looking at the Middle Eastern equivalent of chicken coops. Huh.

Our tour began in Cairo with a stop at the Egyptian museum. What I learned at the museum is that Egyptians like to put things inside of other things. The mummy was placed in a sarcophagus, which was put into another container. Organs such as the lungs, liver, and stomach were sealed in a jar. The coffin was placed inside larger coffins, and all this could be covered with final decorative layers of gold-plated wood. We were also able to see Egyptian shoes, official seals, and ancient jewelry.

I had heard of having one's name inscribed on a cartouche, but I had not realized that its purpose was to help the soul relocate its deceased body. Suddenly, I envisioned myself searching for my body, as though it were a favorite outfit from long ago. It was a strange feeling. Is this how I would feel after death? I developed an urge to look into a mirror and view my physical form as no more than sentimental apparel. It was bizarre.

I learned other things about death at the museum. In Egyptian art, dead Pharaohs are pictured with curved beards or may appear wrapped. Pharaohs, who were depicted while living, have straight beards and perhaps parade one foot in front of the other, as if they are walking. The infamous Gold Room houses the treasures of the Tomb of Tutankhamen. Included in King Tut's showcase is his solid gold funerary mask, inlaid with precious stones. This death mask was actually used to enclose the head of the mummy, within the inner sarcophagus. His gold throne is also on display, along with several of his three nested inner coffins and four outer gilded shrines. In addition to these treasures, other exhibits attested to ancient Egyptian cleverness.

According to our tour guide, Egyptians invented the folding chair. I admired the ancient portable seating device inside the large glass box, accepting that it must have been among the first ever made. Side legs crossed like an 'x,' where central joints allowed the supports to fold closed. Next, our guide informed us that Egyptians had also invented the first folding bed. Before I could digest Egypt's folding mechanisms, she moved onto other ingenuities. Paper, clocks, and the calendar could be accredited to Egypt as well. As she continued to boast, I wondered what China had to say about all this. She proceeded to brag, amid her list of Egyptian grandeurs, that the Nile was the longest river in the world. Taken aback, I was sure that South Americans would profusely disagree, as they revered the Amazon as the longest river. I guess measuring the length of a river is tricky, since scientists have to pinpoint the exact location of the beginning and the end. This is easier said than done, with so many tributaries pouring in and coiling off. Yet, there was no question in her mind. Anyone who disagreed would have been perceived as ignorant. One man did interject, "Well," he started, but she rolled her eyes in response. He took the hint and quieted his concerns. No one cared enough to correct her. After that, she could have told us that Egypt pioneered the first man on the moon, and we wouldn't have confronted her about it. Still, I began taking her assessments with a grain of salt. It was apparent that Egyptian preeminence was slightly elevated in the minds of Egyptians.

Once we made it to Giza, with the great pyramids looming in the distance, I noticed that a caravan of guards and police had joined our bus. The constant presence of men in black suits both comforted and terrified me. I was glad to be protected but scared of the invisible menaces.

The pyramids were astounding. I had always envisioned them in the middle of a desert; in actuality, they are at the edge of one of the largest cities in Africa. It is impossible to imagine how

"Pyramid and Sphinx at Giza"

huge they are, without standing beside them. Their angled sides reached for the sun, and I was dwarfed in comparison to one stone, let alone the millions that formed these wonders. The Great Pyramid has a square base, with each of the four sides measuring around 750 feet long. From ground to apex, it is nearly fifty stories high.

I could not think of a better way to capture the essence of my trip to Egypt than a picture of myself near the pyramids . . . riding a camel. Why not? Well, I *had* read horror stories about this. Accounts were plastered all over the internet. Camel owners would collect a couple dollars from visitors who wanted to get onto their camels. Then, they would escort their customers into the desert, and charge them several hundred dollars to get down. Even Sherry joked about this practice, when someone asked her how much it would cost to ride a camel.

"It is three dollars to get on, and three hundred dollars to get off," she chuckled.

No one in our tour group laughed with her. We had all caught a glimpse of the invisible menace.

Luckily, the men in black did their job. From the time we exited the bus, they had surrounded us, warding off potential scam artists. The camels looked so innocent from a distance, with their wide saddles, woven cloth coverings, and colorful powder-puff tassels. Up close, on the other hand, it was a different experience

"Mounting a Camel"

altogether. They were stinky beasts that alternated between spitting and pooping. The sand was covered with wads of feces. Nevertheless, I was determined to mount one of these animals.

It turned out to be harder to ride a camel than I had imagined. First of all, it is difficult to hoist your leg over their tall backsides, even when they are kneeling. Second, once the camel begins to stand, you feel a little like a pinball. You are hurled forward, as its back legs straighten. Then, you are shot backwards when its front legs extend. I thought I might fall off, more than once. Even on level ground, I felt as though I were teetering. The camel took one clumsy step, and I was finished with the ordeal. I yelled to be let down. The owner hesitated, but the Egyptian FBI stepped in to see that my request was granted. Of course, I had to repeat the process of being whipped across the camel's back in order to descend.

With this feat, I had accomplished everything I had wanted to do in Egypt. I had learned about human history, seen the pyramids of Giza, and ridden a camel (sort of). It had been a good day. Feeling fulfilled, I was not expecting any more excitement.

Thus, my last conversation with Sherry turned out to be an unexpected political and social lesson. Egypt has had the same president, Hosni Mubarak, since 1981. This is not something that most Egyptians are happy about. Our tour guide criticized, "The last election was a play." She dramatically counted on her fingers, as she complained about the people he had run against: 1) someone who was blind, 2) a really old guy on his deathbed, and 3) a man who was going to turn his position over to Mubarak, anyway, if he won. "Against these three, how could he lose?" she protested. I had to laugh, but she didn't crack a smile. This political corruption really infuriated her. I found a new appreciation for the American system of government, despite all its flaws.

Of particular interest to me was the next topic, which was brought up by a man sitting near the middle of the bus. "How do Egyptian people feel about the Israelis?" he had hollered out. Her response caught me off guard.

"We . . . have not . . . been at war for . . . ," she was gritting her teeth a little as she slowly answered.

I am not sure about the rest of her reply, as I, and most of the other people on the bus, burst into laughter. I think she said something about it being over thirty years ago since they had been at war. What a way to answer the question!

"Well, you see, we haven't actively been killing one another officially for decades," I interpreted her words. Her perspective only became more outrageous the more she spoke. She quoted the number of Muslims (80%) and Christians (20%) in percentages of the Egyptian population, but it was like she had the Jews numbered individually.

"There are 2,000 Jews, and these are the old ones that did not leave."

What? Had I heard her correctly? Was she implying that the country *wished* they would leave? I wondered if the Israelis hated the Egyptians this much. Perhaps I would find out. We were sailing into Israel tomorrow, and I was REALLY looking forward to it!

"Dome of the Rock, Jerusalem"

ISRAEL LOVES YOU

What did it mean to be close to God? Like millions of Christians, Jews, and Muslims before me, I was attempting to answer this universal question and strengthen my faith with a pilgrimage to the Holy Land. I was sailing to Israel in an effort to personally unravel the fibers of Christianity through walking in the footsteps of Christ. This was the highlight of my trip. I couldn't wait to become immersed in the land of God . . . to stand where Jesus preached . . . to touch the waters where He was baptized. This was the chance of a lifetime.

As I first stepped onto the arid sands of the country—my head throbbing with itineraries and anticipation—a smiling Jewish man bestowed unto me a radiant white cap embroidered with bright red letters, which read "Israel Loves You." I passed the hat from one hand to the other, examining it. The fabric was stiff with newness, and it smelled of fresh plastic. The color was that of blood-stained letters atop new-fallen snow. This was not what I had expected. It seemed rather strange to distribute hats with such adamant declarations. I quickly stuffed the cap into my backpack and dismissed it.

Our bus tour that day was taking us first to the River Jordan, then atop the Mount of Beatitudes (beside the Sea of Galilee), next to the site of the loaves and fishes miracle, and

"Cap Gift"

finally to a synagogue in the town of Capernaum. Initial stop was the River Jordan! I could hardly wait to dip my toes into the water where John the Baptist had immersed Jesus, as an example to all who accepted salvation. This was going to be the most spiritually meaningful day of my life.

"Directly to our right is the River Jordan," I heard the guide announce. My face shot to the window in order to see the raging waters of the mighty Jordan River. I had always imagined that it would resemble the expansive Ohio or the majestic Mississippi—a swirl of brown current, mixed with reflective sky-blue billows, capable of sweeping away entire houses. Peering through the streaked and spotted glass, all I could see was a narrow line of water, no bigger than a creek. In spots, it wasn't as wide as the branch that ran through our family farm in Kentucky. I could hop across it. For heaven's sake, in places, I believe I could have straddled it. The tall weeds on each side almost pinched the stream out of existence. This was the River Jordan? An official sign before a short bridge confirmed that it was. It was difficult to wrap my mind around, but I gradually accepted that I was looking at the one and only magnificent River Jordan. Well, even though it wasn't as big as I had envisioned, I was still elated at the thought of submerging myself at the place of Christ's baptism.

When we arrived at the site, I practically ran to the baptismal area, rushing past banners of joyous Christians

"River Jordan"

participating in white-robed immersion ceremonies. The river was at one of its widest points here. The muddy waters trickled over cement stairs, which allowed even the feeblest visitors access to its shores. Carefully holding the slick metal rail, I extended one foot into the miry waters below. Cool rivulets surged over the surface of my skin. The sensation was invigorating. I watched the brown waters kiss my creamy complexion before plunging my second foot through the surface and onto the sloshing stairway. The current caressed my ankles and tickled my toes. I loved the feeling of the brisk flow enveloping my feet.

Nonetheless, I would have enjoyed a splash through any refreshing pool within this sunburned landscape. Wasn't a dip in the River Jordan supposed to be more than a casual heat relief? I tried to imagine Jesus standing at the center of the stream, with St. John's hand upon His head. In a single dunk, the road to salvation had been made a little clearer. Unfortunately, the heavens did not open up for me. Not a single dove descended onto my shoulder. What was wrong with me? I was sure that *something* miraculous was supposed to happen. I was supposed to feel closer to God. Wasn't I?

I left the baptismal area for a stroll around the gift shop. Inside, I could purchase a complete holiness package that included an olive wood cross, holy water, anointing oil, holy earth, and frankincense. Perhaps a dozen of these could make me feel closer to God. I bought several sets for friends and family and returned to the bus, my expectations slightly deflated.

The next stop was the Mount of Beatitudes. I hoped that this site would provide a spiritual enlightenment. After all, this was where Jesus preached the Sermon on the Mount. This message was the epitome of Christ's moral teachings. Here He had spoken the Lord's Prayer, the Golden Rule, interpreted the Ten Commandments, and made promises in the Beatitudes. Mourners would be comforted, the hungry would be filled, the meek would inherit the Earth, the merciful would obtain mercy, the pure of heart would see God, and the peacemakers would be called the sons of God. All of this had taken place on these grounds. Surely there was some holiness left for me to absorb.

I sprinted to the top of the hill known as Mount Eremos. There was a Catholic chapel built on the location where the sermon is believed to have been delivered. I entered the tide of people slowly flowing into the church. Halfway inside, I realized that I didn't feel anything beyond claustrophobic and pushed my way back to the freedom of the outdoors. The Sea of Galilee stretched out below me, but it was no more than a meager freshwater lake. Its expanse was so small that I could see across its depths in every direction. I reminded myself that this was where Jesus had instructed Peter to cast out his nets—after a fruitless night of fishing—to receive a bountiful catch as reward for his faith and

"Sea of Galilee"

obedience. This was where Jesus had walked on water to meet his disciples in a perilous storm. The wind and the waves had scared Peter to the point that he had begun to sink before he could meet Christ, and Jesus had mercifully reached out his hand to save him. These fantastic Biblical events had taken place on this humble puddle? This was not at all how I had imagined the Sea of Galilee. Lake Superior had been far more impressive than this legendary Sea. Galilee was an infant in comparison. I suppressed my disappointment and roamed the hillside in an effort to connect with God. Nothing. I began to doubt that I would ever find Him.

For my remaining minutes, I paused to watch the sunlight dance across the glimmering lake. Gentle breezes rushed over the surface, pricking its face with thousands of miniature crests. The shimmering sea was a beautiful contrast to the sandy outcrops that surrounded it—a shining topaz to bejewel the coarsely covered khaki that was Israel. I boarded the bus with increased optimism. Our next stop would be better. So far, I had only been to the place where Jesus' ministry had begun and visited where he had preached. The site of the loaves and fishes was ground zero for an awesome miracle, where Jesus had fed the multitudes. This would be where I would find God. No doubt. In preparation, I rehearsed the story in my mind.

According to the Gospels, Jesus fed over 5,000 people with only five loaves of bread and two fish. After everyone was full, the disciples collected twelve baskets of leftover food. Yes, this had to be an amazing location! I watched the scrubby bushes along the roadway fly past the finger-smeared windows. Finally, I was on my way to someplace special, where God was waiting for me.

I had read about the modern Church of the Multiplication, which had been built on the site of two previous churches to mark the location of the miracle. When Persians destroyed the previous Byzantine church in 614, the exact position of the shrine was lost for nearly 1,300 years. Only after excavations, beginning in the late 1800s, did archeologists discover the mosaic floor of the fifth century church and the older foundation of a smaller fourth century chapel. Today, these mosaics have been brought into the restored structure, along with a large stone that Biblical scholars speculate could have been a platform for the miracle.

I entered the chapel with great reverence and silently approached these precious relics. Any minute, I was hopeful that I would feel the hand of God touch my heart. I would be drawn closer to Him and strengthened with tremendous spiritual wisdom. Standing over the artistic representation of the miracle, I allowed my eyes to internalize the holy images. First, the two fish captured my attention, flanking the bread-filled basket. They were well proportioned, with two dorsal fins opposite a set of pectoral and ventral fins between the head and tail. Indeed, it was extraordinary

"Floor Mosaic Inside Church of the Multiplication"

that Jesus could take only two fish like these and feed so many. Next, I peered into the basket to see the five loaves of bread. To my stark astonishment, there were only four! Where was the fifth loaf? No one had mentioned the absence of the fifth loaf of bread. It was unthinkable that I was the only person to notice this discrepancy, yet the scandal had not been addressed in any of the travel literature. I tried to convince myself that it didn't matter, but somehow it did. If the builders hadn't been able to count the right number of loaves, what made everyone so sure that they had correctly marked the site of the miracle? I felt my spiritual blessing, yet again, slipping away.

I staggered out of the sanctuary, slightly dazed. Had I come all this way for nothing? I felt no closer to God than before I had begun this journey. The Lord had promised to never forsake his children, so why was He turning his back when I was reaching out to know Him? I sat down under an olive tree at the center of the courtyard. Below its sprawling branches the earth was shady. The trunk was twisted and thick, gnarled by decades, or perhaps centuries, of existence. It reminded me of the Tree of Life. But, that was silly! This was not the Tree of Life. It was an old olive tree. Then a small voice in my head whispered, "Does it matter?" I couldn't answer this question. In fact, I was aggravated to consider such an inquiry.

"Olive Tree"

I had one chance left of experiencing the spiritual epiphany that I had come this day to claim. So help me, I was going to walk directly in the footsteps of Christ! The ruins of a synagogue, where Jesus had cast out an unclean spirit, stood in the town of Capernaum. In the fourth chapter of Luke, verses 31-37, the scriptures tell about how He healed and taught the people there on the Sabbath day. If it was true that Jesus had preached and preformed miracles inside this very church, how could I miss being blessed?

The bus pulled up to the gates of the city, and I felt my heart leap within my chest. Pa-pum, pa-pum. A strong, fast beat sent adrenaline racing through my veins. This was it! I was nearly the first person off the bus, and I rocketed toward the ancient structure. All that remained of the synagogue was a maze of columns and partial block walls. I revered the stone floor, thinking, "Jesus must have stepped upon this very spot," but I didn't feel anything. He had to have stood in here somewhere. I paced the area. Like a human dowsing rod, I attempted to locate the footsteps of Christ. Through the doorways, along the wall, around the center of the room, I searched. Where had Jesus stepped? Where was my blessing?

Before I could find it, our time had expired. I felt my heart sink into my stomach. I had journeyed over 6,000 miles to walk in the footsteps of Christ and become closer to God, yet I had failed.

"Ruins at Capernaum"

I couldn't find Him. Something was wrong with me. I boarded the bus for the final time in shame, and I slumped into my seat.

"Would you like to buy a widow's mite?" I heard a cheerful voice ask. I lifted my head in time to see the sparkle in our tour guide's eye. "I'm an archeologist," he shared, "and only about thirty out of every one hundred pieces are worth saving. I sell them for a really good price." I inspected the coin that he held out before me. It was like everything else I had experienced that day, something from the time of Christ that was probably never actually touched by Him. Still, for the first time, I felt an internal tingle. There was a warmth in my heart, as I held this coin and listened to our guide Yossi speak about the widow.

"You know about how she gave the most because she was so poor, even though it was only two mites, compared to the wealth given by the rich men?"

In that moment, I found my blessing. Of course I knew about the pious act of giving from need, rather than from abundance. Even though he was Jewish and I was Christian, we both cherished this Biblical lesson. We had faith that it was true, and that God loved us. I realized that God wasn't in the coin, nor could He be found in a river or a sea or a hillside. I wasn't going to discover Him under a pebble. Our Father can only be found in the hearts of mankind. The fact that we believed in Him and lived our lives, every day, according to His word—this was our path to righteousness.

My mind flashed back to the events of the day. When my heart had rejoiced in the cool waters of the River Jordan, when my eyes had sung praises at the Sea of Galilee, and when I had heard the question under the shelter of the olive tree, these had been the moments when the Lord had reached out to me. Now, I could answer the whisper, "Does it matter?" No, it did not matter where the Tree of Life had stood. It was not important to know the exact location of each miracle. I just had to have faith in them. I did not need to physically walk in the footsteps of Christ. I needed to spiritually use his life as an example for my own. Exhaling in relief, I nodded to confirm that I did know and accept the parable of the widow. My journey had not been in vain after all.

The guide grinned, appreciating our common beliefs. I did purchase a coin from him, but not because of the miniscule chance that it may have passed through the hands of Jesus. On the contrary, I bought the coin because it reminded me to live my life, as the widow did, serving the Lord to the best of my ability.

The next day, I didn't sign up to see the birthplace of Christ or His crucifixion site. There was no need. I had faith that Jesus had been born, crucified, and resurrected. It was not necessary to visit the locales where these events *may* have occurred. I carried the Holy Spirit with me, in my heart, wherever I went.

Instead, I decided to spend my last day in Israel swimming in the Dead Sea. I had a blast! The water was so thick that it was like frolicking in clear corn syrup. I lounged in the salt-saturated liquid as though I were reclining in an invisible lawn chair. It was impossible to sink! The seafloor was covered in spectacular white crystals, which also encircled the entire waterline like a ring of white ice. Temperatures soared toward 100°F, and the sand burned the soles of my feet as I skittered toward the outdoor showers. This was the most fun I had experienced since arriving in Israel. I thanked God for creating the Dead Sea. Also, I praised Him for this country filled with good and loving people.

As we sailed from the shore of Israel that night, I realized that I had possessed the answer all along. Why had it taken me so long to stop looking for God in the things of this world, when I should have been searching for Him in the hearts of men? I pulled the long-forgotten cap from my backpack and read the words aloud, "Israel Loves You," I nodded, and then I added, "and God loves me too . . . wherever I am."

"The Dead Sea"

TURKISH APPLE TEA & MAGIC CARPETS

My childhood could have been the inspiration for a country music charts topper. I was raised to cover my two-piece bikini with a pair of cut-off Levis. The first thing I learned to cook was a pitcher of ice-cold sweet tea. And, my grandparents fended trespassers off our family farm—on more than one occasion—with explosive rounds from a double barrel shotgun. I grew up smelling fragrant pastures of freshly-mowed hay, digging mercilessly at red whelps from poison ivy rashes, and licking sugary nectar from the delicate pistils of honeysuckle flowers. To say that I was a product of the American South would be an atrocious understatement.

Now that I found myself in Kusadasi, Turkey, things were a little different. For starters, there were no two-piece bikinis anywhere in sight. Despite soaring temperatures that would have inspired a skinny-dipping session back home, I was dressed in long sleeves and a skirt that fell below my ankles, in order to blend with local attire. I had even purchased a Hijab, but I felt so silly wearing it to cover my obviously non-Turkish, strawberry-blonde hair that I had to chuckle every time I perched it atop my noggin. It was like wearing a Halloween costume. I tried my best to absorb the liberation that Muslim women say they get from wearing these modest garments. To be judged by characteristics other than appearance was an admirable goal. Try as I may, however, I could

"Henna Tattooing"

not internalize their customs. Everything was so foreign; there wasn't much of their culture that I craved to personally adopt. Appreciate and respect, yes. Take home with me? No. I had no plans of prancing down any street in Kentucky wearing this outfit, sweat pouring from my Hijab-covered head. Just thinking about it made me laugh and cringe simultaneously.

It wasn't only their attire that I struggled to accept. Some of their mannerisms set me on edge. For instance, shaking one's head from side to side, where I come from, means "no"; but in Turkey this gesture communicates, "I don't know." So when a street vendor is offering you some strange concoction and you shake your head in refusal, the salesman believes that you are still thinking it over and pushes that much harder to make a sale. Even more humiliating would be answering a perfectly simple question like, "Are you from Ireland?" with a response of "I don't know." In an effort not to appear mentally challenged, I tried to avoid body language altogether. It was more difficult than I had imagined to stop shaking my head, yet it had been impossible for me to master the successive backward cranial jerking coupled with tongue clicking that signified, "no" in their culture.

I didn't think I was going to personalize any of the Turkish culture, until something totally unexpected happened. What inspired this dramatic turn of events? It all started with a carpet.

"Donner Kabobs Served with Flatbread and Hummus"

I really had wanted to purchase a carpet while in Turkey. It is their trademark export. Yet, I had allowed myself to become sidetracked with swirling brown henna tattoos, döner kebabs served with flatbread and hummus, and wonky looking hookah pipes. Almost every carpet shop entrance showcased an expert weaver, laboriously working the strings of a hand loom like a master harpist. She would robotically weave the interconnected designs for hours, her hands flying over, under, over, and under to pluck the threads through the skeletal warp of a forming tapestry. I had been invited inside by many charismatic Turks on more than one occasion. Until now, my response had been the same: resist shaking my head, smile, and wave goodbye.

If I was really going to buy a rug, it was now or never. My stay in Turkey was coming to an end. For the first time, I accepted an invitation to see the inventory. Downstairs the shop was filled with the musty smells of smoke, wool, and dust. The stale air made it difficult to breathe. It was as if the oxygen itself had been cured in the sun like a vaporous leather. The place was a temple to rugs. The weavings hung as dyed canvases from the walls. You could not look or step without being confronted by a carpet. Not only were they piled into large fabric bricks to cover the floor, but they were also rolled into tight cylinders for further stacking. I followed the store owner, creaking my way up the aged and dimly lit wooden stairway. At the second floor, the atmospheric haze of

"Carpet Shop"

ancient earthiness lifted. The climate was brighter, cooler, and fresher upstairs—the kind of welcoming ambience that inspires shopping.

However, my casual browsing was quickly interrupted with an offer of hot apple tea. A Turkish boy held out a tray filled with small saucers and cups containing a steaming brown liquid. I knew that it would be terribly impolite to refuse, so I selected a cup and removed it from its saucer. The young boy did not move. He held the tray firmly out toward me like a stone statue. Before I could inquire about his demeanor, I felt the near boiling liquid singe my fingertips through the thin chinaware. Immediately, I sat the cup back onto its saucer and retrieved them together. At that, the boy repressed his smile and left. I wondered how many foreign visitors unwittingly burned their fingers on the piping teacups.

Before I could fully contemplate this statistic, I found myself perched on a couch beside an enthusiastic Turkish salesman, who was intent on explaining the symbolism within the hand-woven artworks. Apparently, different motifs can represent anything from a river to fertility. I honestly cannot remember most of the examples he gave me. I do recall that the richest, most long-lasting colors can only be achieved through vegetable dyes, and that carpets enhance their rusty hues with age. Mostly, what I remember from the beginning of our conversation was that he was spewing out moderately interesting facts, and I was annoyed that my tea was too hot to drink, so I was forced to sit and listen to him. By the time my apple tea was barely cool enough to sip, he was showing me photographs of his nomadic family, who had woven some of the rugs he sold. Their simple lifestyle and elaborately decorated camels did spark my curiosity. Who knew you could hang carpets from a camel's hump?

The more my tea cooled, the more captivated I became. There was something about this drink that invited leisurely conversation. The spicy apple smell swirled pleasantly into my nostrils, and the light crisp flavor rolled satisfyingly over my tongue. I enjoyed the clinking sound made when the bottom of the cup hit the top of its slim, matching saucer. Before long, his assistant was displaying one rug after another. He unrolled them, as if each were some sort of magic carpet. Out they tumbled with a flick of his wrists. Threads shimmered like sunlight cascading over water. Tassels flew to greet me.

"How about this one?" he would inquire.

"Well, I like the blue, but I think that the rug is too large," I evaluated.

Within seconds, half a dozen smaller blue rugs were whipped out before me. I patiently slurped my apple tea and noted aspects I liked and disliked in each. With every new wave of magic carpets to consider, the samples grew closer to what I desired. The rug magician could roll and unroll carpets quicker than I thought was humanly possible. Kerslap! Out came another one. "But this one doesn't have any red in it," I critiqued. Thundle, tap. Up it went. Blam! Plop! Two more were presented. One small rug boasted deep blues and rustic reds.

"How much for this one?" I began the negotiations.

"This one is one hundred percent wool and forty years old. It is two hundred and eighty dollars."

I was used to bargaining. I had been trained by master Chinese hagglers. "I will give you two hundred dollars for it," I offered.

"I will take two hundred and fifty dollars," he counter offered.

My tea had been excellent, but it was almost gone. "Two hundred dollars is my highest amount," I cautioned him.

He reached out to shake my hand. As soon as our palms clasped, he smiled and changed the agreement. "Two hundred and thirty dollars," he attempted.

"Two hundred dollars," I corrected him, with my relaxed apple tea smile.

"Okay, okay, two hundred dollars," he agreed.

I left his shop with my rug that day, feeling much happier than I should have about spending two hundred dollars—even if it was on a nicely woven, authentic Turkish carpet. Somehow his soothing apple tea had warmed my heart more than my fingertips.

I had felt at home in his shop of magic carpets, finally discovering a piece of Turkish culture that I desired to make my own. There was something universally human about appreciating another's hospitality through a shared beverage. I had been made to feel like an honored guest, and he had been afforded my undivided attention.

I would not forget this tradition. The following summer, I continued the Turkish business custom. Upon inviting a contractor into my home to discuss the purchase of windows, I considered the best way to make him feel welcomed, while encouraging conversation.

"Would you like an apple drink?" I extended my hospitably.

He accepted. Leaning back comfortably in my porch rocking chairs, we discussed options and prices for the duration of our apple-sipping meeting.

In the end, I love my new windows, but I cherish the memoirs of Turkish Apple Tea and Magic Carpets even more.

LESSONS IN GREEK

The advice given to passengers by the cruise company set the stage for our orientation to mainland Greece. "Don't ask the taxi drivers if they speak English," warned an employee, dressed in a blue-buttoned suit and sailing hat. "They will all answer, 'yes.' Then, you will ask them if they can take you to such-and-such, and they will reply, 'yes.' Finally, once you are zooming away from the dock, you will ask them their name, and they will repeat, 'yes.' Instead, your first question should be something completely off-the-wall, like, 'Do you think it's going to snow today?' If they say 'yes,' keep on walking!"

We had already been scammed several times in Santorini, when we hadn't heeded the tourist warnings. Orally advertised restaurant "specials," like our cactus juice and baklava, were only special for the owner, who collected upwards of fifty dollars a snack. Sure, the panoramic cliff views had been phenomenal, but if I had it to do over, I would have definitely consulted a price-revealing menu. I hated to be taken advantage of. Yet, it kept happening. While buying perfume, the man behind the register tried to charge me €13. When I complained that €5 plus €4 totaled €9 and counted it out on my fingers in front of him, he reluctantly accepted my ten Euro note. Had he expected me to pay without thinking?

"Fifty Dollar Greek 'Special' of Cactus Juice and Baklava"

On a separate occasion, an older Greek man refused to sell me coins when I had argued with him about changing the price mid purchase. He had increased the cost from ten coins for a Euro to that much a piece. It seemed that if you could think of a way to get cheated, the Greeks had already thought of it . . . and they had been perfecting it for centuries. Staying ahead of them was a daunting challenge.

I had come to Greece to learn at the birthplace of academia. Socrates, Plato, and Aristotle had revolutionized philosophy, impacting science and education the world over. As a teacher myself, I had wanted to glean some knowledge from this land of scholars. So far, I was only learning how to get ripped off.

A short €7 ride from our hotel would take us to the Acropolis. Of course, the taxi driver charged us an extra €3 for the hotel call fee, which I do not believe is standard practice. Regardless, we did make it to the ancient city on the hill. The views were spectacular. All of modern Athens lay at my feet. The valley was a sea of white cubed dwellings mixed with green patches of trees. Walking up to the settlement was like traveling back in time. Life in ancient Greece was so easy to imagine, when surrounded by the buildings of the period.

My favorite structure was the Erechtheum because of the porch of the Caryatids. The temple was constructed a little after 400 B.C., with six robed women carved from stone serving as

"Erechtheum with the Porch of the Caryatids"

columns. Each one was slightly different. The draping of the garments across the torso was unique for every statue, and some protruded their left leg, while others bent their right. It was amazing how their elegantly slender necks supported tons of marble ceiling above their heads.

I couldn't understand why the Parthenon was the most famous of the temples. To me, Erechtheum was much more breathtaking. Maybe it was because the Parthenon had been built to honor Athena, the protector of Greece, or, perhaps, because it epitomized classic Greek architecture, with its proportions approximating the golden ratio. I didn't know. What further confused me, however, was all the scaffolding surrounding the Parthenon. I didn't learn about the tragic tale until after we had left the Acropolis and entered a local shop. As related by the store owner, the government was selling ancient columns to museums and replacing them with fake columns! Would the Greeks stop at nothing to make a buck?

On our way back to the hotel, our latest taxi driver invented an Athens Tax to explain why our fare would cost over €30, instead of the original €7 it had taken to get there. By now, I knew that he was lying, but what do you do? I decided to pay the bill and add him to my long list of Greek con artists.

I was fed up! I vowed to never return to Greece.

"Parthenon with Scaffolding and Cranes"

All this trickery reminded me of one of the most famous Greek stories, The Trojan Horse. I know that historians are still debating about whether a giant horse, filled with soldiers, was actually given as a gift during the Trojan War, but I don't have to think twice. Greeks were sneaky swindlers! Like I said before, if you could think of a way that you might get duped, the Greeks had already thought of it . . . and perfected it.

Fortunately, I did learn my ultimate Greek lesson: Φοβοῦ τοὺς Δαναοὺς καὶ δῶρα φέροντας (*Phobou tous Danaous kai dōra pherontas*), which translates, "Beware of the Greeks, even bearing gifts." Although this was not the lesson I had originally set out to learn in Greece, I accepted the truism.

"Views from the Greek Islands"

RETURNING HOME

Three weeks is long enough for me to be away from home. When I start thinking nostalgically about Vanceburg, I know it's time to head back. I missed my house. I wanted to watch a scary movie, and I longed for rain. Yes, that's correct. The entire time we had been gone it hadn't rained once! I like rain—the way it cools the air and makes everything smell so fresh. Thunder is also my favorite sound, and I missed that too. The weather in the Mediterranean is hot, dry, and sunny, with a chance of wind. In fact, I perspired so profusely in the arid environment that, despite drinking over a gallon of water every day, I rarely had to pee. Can you imagine that? It's so interesting the secrets that you uncover when you travel. Overall, I had learned a great deal.

In Germany, I had visited the land of my ancestors and discovered much about where I had come from and why I developed into the person that I am today. Crossing Italy, I fed my artistic soul with the waters of Venice and the masterpieces of Rome. From the base of the Egyptian pyramids, I sifted through human history to better understand my place. Within the oasis of Israel, I refreshed my spiritual being and further developed my perspective of life. I experienced a culmination of culture in the rich country of Turkey, adding fuel to an already glowing passion for travel. From Greece, I learned a vital lesson in the land of educators, scholars, and philosophers. I had experienced more on this journey than I could have ever imagined.

Definitely, I had learned a lot about diversity and witnessed the tension that these differences sometimes create. The Arabs—I had observed—despised the Jews, and the Jews thought little of the Arabs. Although I had known this intellectually, I had never before experienced the discourse firsthand. I will never forget the comment made by one Jewish man as he pointed to a trash-filled Arab camp. "Do you know the reason they live in shacks like that?" he had taunted. "It's so that they can pick up and move over a little when they get infested with fleas." I hadn't been sure if he was joking or not, but the underlying point was understood. Jews and Arabs did not get along. This fact had been etched into my consciousness, no longer merely a television sound bite.

Moreover, I imagined that neither group would meld well with the Greeks. People in the Middle East, regardless of religion, dressed conservatively. What would an Egyptian woman, who wore a full burka, think about Greece's topless beaches? Even I had been annoyed by a postcard, picturing an exposed breast in the foreground of the Acropolis. "I went all the way to Greece, and all I saw was a nipple!" I had blurted out my latest slogan for the country. My exasperation had been so fitting, that Chad had actually asked if the card had really said that. Ha! I would speculate that an Islamic woman would have been even further disgusted.

I was glad that, as an American, I possessed enough tolerance to drift from one culture to the next, learning from each. I gleaned what I liked, and left the rest where I found it. I had gathered the hospitality of Turkey (offered with spicy apple tea), for instance, while leaving the Trojan horse in Greece. I had thoroughly enjoyed myself, traveling from Europe to Africa to the Middle East without major incident. I was, however, delighted to be returning to the land of the free and the home of the brave.

From Germany's "auf wiedersehen" to Greece's "αντίο," I bid you farewell.

"Me with My Hijab and Henna Tattoo"

ACKNOWLEDGEMENTS

I would like to thank my family and friends for their support, assistance, and encouragement in making this book a reality. Special thanks to the following people:

Chad Darland

Barbara Stone

Sarah Stone Mawk

Michael Reis

Wanda Sullivan

Jenny Sullivan

Clarence Stone (1953-2007)

"My Family"

Useful Phrases for the

Fly-by-night Traveler Headed to the Mediterranean

Italian:

Hello.	Ciao.	*[chow]*
Please.	Per favore.	*[pehr fah-voh-reh]*
Thank you.	Grazie.	*[graht-zee-eh]*
You're welcome.	Prego.	*[preh-goh]*
Yes.	Sì.	*[see]*
No.	No.	*[noh]*
Sorry.	Mi dispiace.	*[mee dee-spyah-cheh]*
Goodbye.	Arrivederci.	*[ah-ree-vuh-dehr-chee]*

Useful Phrases for the

Fly-by-night Traveler Headed to the Mediterranean

(CONTINUED)

Arabic (Egypt):

Hello.	سلام	*[salam]*
Please.	من فضلك	*[min fadlak (m)/ fadlik (f)]*
Thank you.	شكرا	*[shukran]*
You're welcome.	ألعفو	*[al'afw]*
Yes.	ل	*[aiwa]*
No.	نعم	*[na'am]*
Sorry.	أسف!	*[aasef]*
Goodbye.	مع السلامة	*[ma'a salama]*

Useful Phrases for the

Fly-by-night Traveler Headed to the Mediterranean

(CONTINUED)

Hebrew (Israel):

Hello.	שלום	*[shalom]*
Please.	בבקשה	*[bevakasha]*
Thank you.	רב תודות	*[rav todot]*
You're welcome.	בבקשה	*[bevakasha]*
Yes.	אל	*[ken]*
No.	ךכ	*[lo]*
Sorry.	סליחה!	*[slicha]*
Goodbye.	להתראות	*[lehitraot]*

Useful Phrases for the

Fly-by-night Traveler Headed to the Mediterranean

(CONTINUED)

Turkish:

Hello.	Merhaba.	*[mar-ha-ba]*
Please.	Lütfen.	*[loot-fen]*
Thank you.	Teşekkür ederim.	*[ter-shek-ewr edehrem]*
You're welcome.	Bir şey degil.	*[ber-sha-dighl]*
Yes.	Evet.	*[ehveht]*
No.	Hayir.	*[hah-ir]*
Sorry.	Üzgünüm.	*[yuz-googn]*
Goodbye.	Hoşça kal.	*[hohshta cowl]*

Useful Phrases for the

Fly-by-night Traveler Headed to the Mediterranean

(CONTINUED)

Greek:

Hello.	Γειά σας.	*[ya sas]*
Please.	παρακαλώ.	*[parakaló]*
Thank you.	Ευχαριστώ.	*[efharistó]*
You're welcome.	παρακαλώ.	*[parakaló]*
Yes.	Ναι.	*[ne]*
No.	όχι.	*[ohi]*
Sorry.	Συγνώμη!	*[sygnómi]*
Goodbye.	Γειά σας.	*[yiá sas]*

Mediterranean Menu

Italian Bruschetta

Egyptian Raspberry Mint Drink

Israeli Rice with Black Beans and Chickpeas

Turkish Döner Kebab

Greek Baklava

(Use the recipes on the following pages to create a Mediterranean meal, and bring a little of these cultures into your own home.)

Italian Bruschetta

Ingredients

- 1½ cups Roma tomatoes, cubed
- 2 Tablespoons red onion, diced
- 1 garlic clove, chopped
- 2 Tbsp. fresh basil, chopped
- ½ teaspoon red wine vinegar
- 2½ Tablespoons olive oil
- 1 dash salt and pepper
- ½ loaf long French bread, sliced
- ¼ teaspoon garlic salt

Preparation

1) Chop Roma tomatoes, red onion, and garlic.
2) Put into medium sized bowl.
3) Chop basil until fine, and add to bowl.
4) Add red wine vinegar and 1 Tablespoon oil.
5) Salt and pepper; mix well.
6) Refrigerate for 1 hour.
7) When ready to serve, preheat broiler and slice bread into 1-inch slices on 45-degree angle.
8) Combine remaining 1½ Tablespoons of oil with garlic salt.
9) Brush entire surface of bread (both sides) with olive oil mixture.
10) Broil bread slices in oven for 1½ to 2 minutes per side or until browned.
11) Centrally plate refrigerated tomato mixture and arrange bread around like spokes.

Egyptian Raspberry Mint Drink

Ingredients

- 1 bunch fresh mint
- 2½ cups pineapple juice
- 1 cup frozen raspberries
- 3 ounces frozen limeade concentrate, thawed
- 1 liter cold carbonated lemon-lime beverage
- lime wedge, to garnish (optional)

Preparation

1) Rub the mint leaves around the inside of a pitcher; then drop a few into each glass and place the rest into the bottom of the pitcher.
2) Pour into pitcher the pineapple juice, raspberries, limeade, and carbonated beverage; mix well.
3) Serve with a lime wedge on the edge of the glass.

Israeli Rice with Black Beans and Chickpeas

Ingredients

- ½ Tablespoon olive oil
- 1 small clove garlic, minced
- ½ cup uncooked basmati rice
- 1 teaspoon ground cumin
- 1 teaspoon ground coriander
- ½ teaspoon ground turmeric
- ½ teaspoon ground cayenne pepper
- 1 (15 oz.) can chicken stock
- 1 (15 oz.) can garbanzo beans (chickpeas), drained and rinsed
- 1 (15 oz.) can black beans, drained and rinsed
- ½ bunch chopped fresh cilantro (optional)
- ½ bunch chopped fresh parsley (optional)
- 1 oz. pine nuts (optional)
- salt to taste
- ground black pepper to taste

Preparation

1) Heat olive oil in a large saucepan over medium heat.
2) Stir in garlic, and cook 1 minute.
3) Stir in rice, cumin, coriander, turmeric, and cayenne pepper.
4) Cook and stir 5 minutes; then pour in chicken stock.
5) Increase heat, and bring to a boil.
6) Reduce heat to low, cover, and simmer 20 minutes.
7) Gently mix the garbanzo beans and black beans into cooked rice, along with optional ingredients if you desire: cilantro, parsley, and pine nuts.
8) Season with salt and pepper.

Turkish Döner Kebab

Ingredients

- 1 lb. leg of lamb, boned & sliced
- ½ Tablespoon black pepper
- 1 lb. ground lamb
- ¾ cup olive oil (extra for frying)
- 1 egg
- 1 Tablespoon salt
- onions, processed until a liquid (1½ cups)

Preparation

1) Remove any bits of skin and bone from the meat, and cut into serving-size pieces (about 1-inch cubes). Pound with a meat tenderizer until thin (¼ to ½-inch thick). Trim fat. Slice into inch squares.
2) Prepare a marinade of onion juice in food processor; pour into bowl.
3) Add ½ cup olive oil, salt, and pepper to onion juice; soak meat in marinade in refrigerator overnight.
4) With hands, mix ground lamb and egg; then refrigerate.
5) After marinating, remove meat from marinade and coat with remaining ¼ cup olive oil.
6) Thread pieces of meat onto skewers, starting with the larger pieces.
7) Adhere a coating of ground lamb mixture, molding it onto skewer.
8) Fry covered in oiled pan over medium heat, until meat is cooked.
9) Drain and dry pan.
10) Add 1-2 Tablespoons of olive oil to pan, heat, and brown both sides of kebabs over medium-high heat.

Greek Baklava

Ingredients

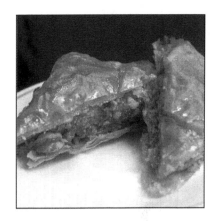

- 1 (16 oz.) pkg. phyllo dough
- 1-1¼ cup butter, melted
- ½ pound chopped nuts
- 1 teaspoon ground cinnamon
- 1 cup water
- 1 cup white sugar
- 1 teaspoon vanilla extract
- ½ cup honey

Preparation

1) Preheat oven to 350°F. Melt 1 cup butter. Brush some butter onto the bottom and sides of a 9x13-inch pan.

2) If nuts are not chopped, crush by beating them with a rolling pin inside a zipper bag; then toss with cinnamon. Set aside.

3) Unroll phyllo dough. Cut whole stack in half to fit pan. Cover phyllo with a dampened cloth to keep from drying out as you work.

4) Place a sheet of dough in pan, butter top of every sheet thoroughly. Repeat until you have 8 sheets layered. Sprinkle 2-3 Tablespoons of nut mixture on top. Add another sheet of dough, butter, nuts, layering as you go. Top with 6-8 sheets of dough (buttered in between).

5) Using a sharp knife, cut into squares all the way to the bottom of the pan by making 3 vertical cuts and 4 horizontal cuts. Then, make diagonal cuts to turn squares into triangles. Bake for about 50 minutes or until baklava is golden and crisp.

6) In the meantime, make sauce while baklava is baking. Boil sugar and water until sugar is melted. Add vanilla and honey. Reduce heat and simmer for about 20 minutes.

7) Remove baklava from oven and immediately spoon sauce over it. Let cool. Serve in cupcake papers. These freeze well, but leave uncovered, as they get soggy if wrapped.

ABOUT THE AUTHOR

I am a teacher, an artist, a writer, and an avid traveler. Born and raised in the Ohio River Valley of Northeastern Kentucky, I have grown accustomed to rural life and strong community ties. Since I was a little girl, I have been consumed by the drive to create, with a burning determination to always "make something."

After graduating as valedictorian of my high school class, I attended Morehead State University to obtain my Bachelor of Arts in elementary education and art, and I earned my Master of Arts in art education through the University of Cincinnati. Through the Continuing Education Option, I became a certified Rank I teacher in the state of Kentucky.

Presently, I am a tenured visual arts educator at Central Elementary in my hometown of Vanceburg, Kentucky. Teaching children to draw, paint, and create other types of art has helped me to refine and improve my own artistic skills, while sharing techniques with younger artists. Similarly, assisting children in writing has allowed me to enhance my own narrative style. From experience, I have learned that the best way to learn is to teach.

In my spare time, I enjoy traveling and have had the opportunity to visit many places throughout the world, including China, Japan, Mexico, Canada, Jamaica, Antigua, Dominican Republic, Puerto Rico, Kiribati, Brazil, Paraguay, Argentina, Norway, France, England, Ireland, and Scotland. These travels have had a profound impact on my art, teaching, and writing. I find other people's way of life, customs, and traditions fascinating.

Thank you for taking the time to read my book. I hope that you found something of interest, insight, or humor. Most definitely, I believe that all people should learn to laugh at their own quirks and make an effort to experience customs outside their norm. Life can be a great mix of education and fun!

Made in the USA
San Bernardino, CA
08 March 2015